THE
BIBLE AND
SCIENCE

UNITY NOT OPPOSITION

EDDIE D. LEACH, PH. D

WESTBOW·
PRESS
A DIVISION OF THOMAS NELSON
& ZONDERVAN

WestBow Press books may be ordered through booksellers or by contacting:

WestBow Press
A Division of Thomas Nelson & Zondervan
1663 Liberty Drive
Bloomington, IN 47403
www.westbowpress.com
1 (866) 928-1240

ISBN: 978-1-4908-5388-8 (sc)
ISBN: 978-1-4908-5389-5 (hc)
ISBN: 978-1-4908-5387-1 (e)

Library of Congress Control Number: 2014917420

Printed in the United States of America.

WestBow Press rev. date: 10/01/2014

CONTENTS

PREFACE

Why I Wrote This Book

After many years of teaching science in the college and university setting and after many years of membership in the Christian Church/Churches of Christ of the Restoration Movement, I am very troubled and perplexed over the various mindsets and opinions in the scientific and religious communities regarding the teachings of the Bible and the discoveries of science and the wonders of God's creation.

It seems that there are three main, diametrically opposed groups at war with each other, creating a *dilemma* for human kind.

The Dilemma

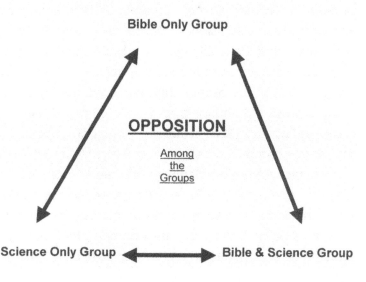

The **Bible Only Group** is made up of those individuals who believe that the creation of the entire universe was done by Jehovah God in six, twenty-four hour days in approximately 4004 BC. This makes the universe a little over 6000 years old. (4004 BC plus AD 2014 equals 6018 years). This discipline teaches very plainly that God was responsible for the creation of the universe and all its components. It doesn't explain in any detail *how* all of this was accomplished, but it certainly does tell us *who* did it.

The **Science Only Group** is made up of those who have studied extensively one or more of the many fields of science, i. e., biology, geology, paleontology, chemistry, physics, mathematics, astronomy, anthropology, and on and on. Through scientific discoveries made over the past few centuries, a different point of view has arisen. Members of this group believe that the origin of the universe and all its components came into existence over a much longer period of time -- billions of years. Through their observations and discoveries, they've put together a roadmap or flow chart describing the events in order of their occurrence. They seem to believe that all matter, life forms, energy, space, and time came into existence without any origin or intervention by a supreme being. Most probably do not even believe in the existence of a supreme being. Their charts do not tell *who* did it, but they are telling us *how* it was done.

The **Bible + Science Group** is made up of individuals who've studied both the Bible and science. Members of this group, of which I am one, believe that the teachings of the Bible and the discoveries of science should not contradict each other since both have the same origin—God. They believe that many authors were inspired by God to express His thoughts and actions, and these authors then wrote the books of Bible to make a permanent record of them. Members of this group also believe that the study and discoveries of Science depict the power, planning, and majesty of God, just as the Bible does. Since both the Bible and science have their origins in God, there should be no discrepancies or inconsistencies between them. Just as a Bible student can use one part of the Bible to help understand another part, one should be able to use the Bible to help understand and explain science and use science to help understand and explain the Bible, because both of are *true revelations from God to man when properly interpreted.*

God is not going to lie to or mislead His children. He is always truthful to us whether He is speaking to us through the Bible or through science. If one perceives differences between the Bible and science, both of which are true, then the problem lies in the incorrect interpretation of one or the other of God's revelations to us, or perhaps some of each. Knowing God is a constantly ongoing process of learning and discovery both in science and in biblical studies. Neither science nor biblical learning has all the answers. Is it even possible, much less probable, that we will ever completely know or understand the entire mind of God in our lifetimes?

There are differences in the *purpose* of the Bible and science, however. The Bible isn't a science text and scientific knowledge isn't the Bible. The Bible explains God's plan of how His people should live to glorify Him, how to have their sins forgiven, and how to be reconciled to Him. God, who created science, has given us the ability to pursue scientific learning and discover His almighty power, majesty, and knowledge. This endeavor will make our lives much better if used correctly, or much worse if used incorrectly. For example, medicine has relieved untold death and suffering, while modern weapons of mass destruction have caused an immeasurable amount of death and suffering. Our lives are much more comfortable today with the earthly conveniences made possible through science.

But, while science doesn't reveal any plan for our salvation or the proper relationship we should have with the Creator, it certainly does show the power, majesty, and supremacy of God. This aspect alone should help reinforce our faith in Him and hopefully help us realize that He cares for us and has a plan for each of our lives. It's through careful study of *both the Bible and science* that we can more completely know and understand all of His knowledge and revelations to us.

This concept tells both *who* created and *how* it was done.

Some points to ponder:

Is this dilemma part of God's plan and does it reflect His wishes for humankind?

What is the cause or origin of these differences in beliefs and opinions?

Should these differences be resolved?

Can these differences be resolved? If they can be resolved, how?

What harm is done if they aren't resolved?

Are some of God's children being misled or confused by these differences?

Will some of God's children lose their salvation because of this dilemma?

Who will be responsible for the loss of their salvation?

What will be the fate of those who mislead some of *God's **little ones***?

As Jesus said,

> But if anyone causes one of these **little ones** who believe in me to sin, it would be better for him to have a large millstone hung around his neck and to be drowned in the depths of the sea. (Matt. 18:6 NIV)

> And if anyone causes one of these **little ones** who believe in me to sin, it would be better for him to be thrown into the sea with a large millstone tied around his neck. (Mark 9:42 NIV)

Who has the responsibility to make sure that they are teaching others the truth?

Do your best to present yourself to God as one approved, a workman who does not need to be ashamed and who correctly handles the word of truth. (2 Tim 2:15 NIV)

Since the New Testament Canon didn't exist when these words were written, could Paul have been inspired to use the phrase, *word of truth*, to mean everything God has revealed and *will reveal* to humankind, not only through a study of His words (the Bible), but through a study of His works (creation) as well? Is it possible to get the complete picture God is giving us by studying *only a part* of His revelation to us? Hopefully this book will help illustrate the need to *combine* and *unify* these two revelations. It's not an easy process because it has so many different facets that must be studied, analyzed, interpreted, and considered.

It's important to keep in mind that *all the data is not in.* There's always continued study and discovery in both Bible knowledge and scientific research. Therefore, these areas of study must be continually revisited and restudied as new discoveries are made in each discipline in order to stay informed of *everything* God is revealing to us.

I hope to use this book to present a logical sequence of some of the material I have collected during more than sixty years of careful study, research, meditation, and prayer. It hasn't been an easy project and is one that will *never* be completely finished because of the new discoveries that are made on a daily basis in science and in God's written Word.

It's my fervent hope and prayer that this book will help *unify* God's words and works in our understanding and that it will *strengthen* our faith and dedication to Him and His purpose in our lives. I'm sure that God will welcome the strengthening of our faith and the increased dedication of our lives to Him.

My prayer is:

Please, Dear Lord God, do not let these words weaken any reader's faith in You. Instead, may they serve to strengthen their knowledge of You, to increase their faith in You, to understand just how much You love us, and to know that You have real purpose for each of our lives.

Amen

INTRODUCTION

A Parable

Jesus used parables very effectively in many of His teachings. Good parables are very easily understood and can convey quickly and clearly the principles the teacher desires. I would like to use the following parable that, hopefully, will illustrate a principle somewhat difficult to explain otherwise.

> Johnny, a young boy about eight years old, came home from school one day and went into the kitchen where his mom was busy preparing dinner for the family. After a few moments of the usual conversation between the two concerning the day's activities, Johnny asked, "Mom, where did I come from?"
>
> Mom had been expecting a question of this type since the boy was at that age when he probably was hearing things at school to prompt his curiosity. Still, she was somewhat stunned, and not really prepared to respond at that exact moment, so she said, "Why don't you ask your dad when he gets home from work." This would allow her to forewarn dad concerning Johnny's question and allow him time to prepare a proper answer. A little later, dad came home and Mom privately informed him about the question Johnny was going to ask him.
>
> The family gathered for the evening meal and had the usual conversations. When the meal was over and Mom was clearing the table, dad said to Johnny, "Mom says you have a question for me?" Johnny replied in the

affirmative, so dad suggested the two of them go into the den where they could talk.

Dad had been looking forward to the opportunity of answering this question from his son since he was a physician specializing in human reproduction, obstetrics, gynecology, and problems in fertility in both males and females. Because mom had alerted him about the question, he had time to gather some of the textbooks, charts, and teaching aids he'd collected and used in his practice of medicine, and in teaching these subjects at the nearby medical school. Needless to say, he was more than adequately prepared to answer Johnny's question.

When the two of them arrived in the den, dad asked, "So, Johnny, what's your question?

Johnny hesitantly responded, "Dad, where did I come from?"

Dad expressed his pleasure that Johnny had come to him for the answer to an important question like this, and then launched into a detailed explanation that would confuse even a third year medical student. Dad wanted to give his *best* effort to answer his son accurately and completely so he held nothing back.

He began with the explanation of gametogenesis (spermatogenesis and oogenesis) including the formation of the haploid number of chromosomes in order to allow the return to the diploid number following fertilization of the ovum by the spermatozoan. He went on to explain the stages of embryogenesis from the zygote through the morula, blastula, and gastrula stages, to form the triploblastic embryo; then he went on to explain the formation of the extra-embryonic membranes: the amnion, chorion, allantois, and yolk sac. Next he explained the formation of the placenta from part of the chorion and the allantois with chorionic villi penetrating into the endometrium of the mother's uterus so as to allow nutrients, oxygen, carbon dioxide, and waste products to be exchanged between the mother's and baby's circulatory systems. Thus far, the answer had taken about an hour of time and utilized many diagrams, charts, and pictures, yet, he'd covered only a brief outline of what he knew about the subject.

At this point, Dad took a deep breath and paused to see how Johnny was grasping his explanation thus far and ask if he had any questions. The expression on Johnny's face was a sight to behold. It was very clear to Dad that Johnny had *no idea* what he was talking about. (Perhaps some of you reading this may have about the same facial expression as Johnny had.)

Johnny was simply too young and incapable of understanding what Dad was trying to explain. Dad's words just weren't in Johnny's vocabulary. (Can't you imagine the expression on Dad's face if God were to lecture him on what He knew about the subject? I'll bet Dad couldn't even *begin* to understand all that God could teach him either.)

Dad now realized that his answers, accurate and detailed as they were, were more confusing to Johnny than being of any help at this point of his development and knowledge. He realized that his answer to Johnny's simple question concerning his origin needed to be one simple enough to be comprehended by Johnny at this point, yet it needed to be truthful and accurate so that he would not be confused when he grew older and was presented with more detailed and complex answers. In short, the answer needed to be an accurate, truthful outline upon which more information could be added as needed when he could better understand.

After a moment of thought, Dad responded, "Johnny, God made you."

Johnny's face immediately showed comprehension and relief. He understood *that* answer. It was simple and adequate for his need at that time.

Dad explained that as Johnny matured, he could answer the more complex concepts that his son then would be able to understand. Johnny seemed quite relieved and satisfied.

I'm using this parable because I believe it applies to the time when humans first asked God, "Where did we come from?" The Trinity (God the Father, Christ the Son, and the Holy Spirit) could have given an infinitely detailed answer to the humans They had created. Instead, They knew at that point in time humans just weren't ready to understand or grasp their explanations. Like Johnny, the human beings of that time didn't have the vocabulary or ability to understand the detailed explanation They could have given. Instead, The Trinity simply answered, through Moses in the book of Genesis, "I (We) made you!", and gave some brief information about how They did it. Even today, we still aren't capable of understanding everything The Trinity is revealing to as we continually study nature and creation and their relationships to our study of Scripture.

God knew that as humans became increasingly curious and knowledgeable about His universe, He could reveal to them, in greater and greater detail, the processes involved in it's creation. What might be His plan for the revelations He would provide us and how would He bring it about? Could it be, as we continue our study of science, God is progressively revealing to us His creative processes? Perhaps this is a part of the *mystery* referred to so many times in the Bible and covered later in Chapter 3 entitled God's Mystery.

Another example illustrating this point was in a recent Sunday comics section of a local newspaper. It showed a mother and her young daughter taking a walk on a beautiful autumn day. The little girl was entranced as she looked at the millions of beautifully colored leaves falling to the ground and the equally beautiful leaves still remaining on the trees. The little girl said that she knew why the leaves were so beautiful and asked her mother if she knew why. The mother said that she did know and went on to explain that all spring and summer the leaves made food for the tree but when the weather gets cold the trees go to sleep and don't need the food any more, so the trees cut off supplying nourishment to their leaves. Without this nourishment, the leaves begin to die causing chemical changes in the leaves that produce the colors. These colors vary as time passes and are different in the many different kinds of trees. The little girl appeared to be puzzled and confused as she said "Oh, but Grandma said that God paints them one by one." Now the mother had the puzzled expression. Both explanations were correct, but how would she explain that to her daughter? One explained **who** while the other explained **how**.

In another cartoon a little child is standing on the rim of what appears to be the Grand Canyon in Arizona. The child is telling his parents, "The park ranger just said that the canyon was formed by the river washing away the soil and rock until the canyon is like it is today. But my Sunday school teacher said that God made it." Isn't this another example of one answer explaining **who** while the other explains **how**?

If God had chosen to reveal *all* the details of His creative process to Moses, he probably would still be writing the book of Genesis to this day, with no end in sight, even if he had access to a computer with a word-processing program.

CHAPTER 1

The Importance Of True Testimony

It's very important, if not essential, for one's testimony to correlate with all the physical evidence related to that testimony. In other words, what one says and what one does must corroborate and correlate with each other. If they don't, either or both of them are liable to be questioned as being completely truthful and accurate. As others have said, "It is important to w*alk the walk, and talk the talk.*"

The following two stories are very simple examples that, hopefully, will illustrate this point. In the first example, there is an ulterior motive on the part of the suspect to the extent that he lied repeatedly, hoping to protect himself. The evidence surrounding the incident overwhelmingly proved his deception and guilt. In the second incident, the evidence seemed to be at odds with the known facts *at a point in time.* There was never any attempt to hide something or deceive anyone. It was just a matter of revealing more of the known facts at the appropriate time for the benefit of all the parties involved. The contrast between the two examples points out that the first was concocted for a selfish self-protective purpose. The second was done in a loving "need to know" basis, and the full truth was revealed when the time was right and for the benefit of all involved.

Example 1:

A very expensive porcelain figurine was taken during a home burglary. The owner of the house, from which the object was taken, returned home unexpectedly and noticed a person fleeing from his house as he pulled into his driveway. He used his cell phone to call 911. The dispatcher radioed a police car that just happened to be patrolling the neighborhood. The police quickly responded and spotted a suspicious looking person in the area. They noticed him dropping something in a trash container when he saw the police car and began to run. They apprehended the person and questioned him about his behavior. The suspect testified that he did not do anything unlawful. The police went to the trash container and recovered the object the suspect had dropped there. It was later identified by the homeowner as a porcelain figurine belonging to him and kept in the same room that later was determined to be the burglar's point of entry. Also, it was the same room from which the owner saw the suspect fleeing. The police showed the figurine to the apprehended person. He said that he did not steal it and furthermore that he had never seen it before.

The police took the suspect and the figurine to police headquarters. Upon forensic examination, they found the suspect's fingerprints in several places on the figurine as well as some fresh blood. The police also observed that the apprehended person had a bleeding cut on one of his fingers. Further analysis showed that the blood DNA on the figurine was the same as that of the suspect.

In short, the suspect's testimony didn't correlate with the physical evidence. If you were a juror in the criminal case brought against this person, which would you tend to believe more, his testimony or the physical evidence? The verbal testimony of the suspect clearly did not fit the physical evidence. It was obvious that the suspect was lying. The sole purpose of his testimony was to attempt to protect himself for very selfish reasons.

Example 2:

Several years ago a college professor was conducting his laboratory class in Anatomy and Physiology for nursing students in a Christian liberal arts college. This particular laboratory involved the examination and analysis of blood. The students collected their own blood from finger sticks and used the equipment available in the laboratory to determine the hematocrit, hemoglobin concentration, red cell count, white cell count, differential white cell count and blood type.

The lab went smoothly with no significant problems and all but one of the students had finished the exercise by the end of the lab period at 5 pm. The one remaining student was a girl, whom we shall call Mary. Mary was becoming increasingly upset as she repeatedly ran and re-ran the test for her blood type. The professor noticed Mary's concern and asked what the problem was. Mary said she couldn't get the right results for her blood type. She said she knew she was blood type O, but the only results she got indicated she was blood type A. Something had to be wrong.

The professor thought that perhaps the blood typing serum might've been contaminated by repeated use during the class period and somehow that had caused this student's "erroneous" results. The professor had fresh, unopened bottles of blood typing serum and gave them to the frustrated student. He watched her to make sure that she did the procedures for the blood test properly. The results were the same. Mary definitely had type A blood. So, what could be wrong?

The professor inquired if Mary believed her blood type was O from previous testing or blood donations. She answered "No, but I know that both my parents are type O because it was on both of the blood donor cards they received when they donated blood." She became even more upset when she asked whether her recollection of the genetics of blood types they had covered a few days earlier was correct. She asked that if both her parents are type O, then she would *have to be* type O also? The professor replied, "Yes, your recollection is correct. If your parents are both type O, then you would have to be type O as well."

The clearly distraught student said, "But these tests show I'm type A. *How can that be?*"

The answer was obvious. At least one of her parents did not have type O blood and that at least one of her parents was not her true biological parent. The physical data clearly did not agree with or support her concept of her biological parentage.

"But my dad is a minister and my mom is deeply involved in church work!" she said. "How could this have happened?" It was a very embarrassing time for both Mary and the professor as each one silently considered the several possible explanations.

Mary left the lab to go to her dorm, clearly carrying the world on her shoulders. She had indisputable proof that at least one of her parents was not her true biological parent as she had believed all her life. One can only imagine the shock, frustration, doubt, suspicion, and probably a myriad of other emotions she was feeling at this time.

The blood lab had taken place on Thursday afternoon. On Friday morning, the class met again for lecture. The professor was wondering whether Mary would even be in class, and if so, what her state of mind would be. When the professor walked into the lecture hall, there was Mary sitting in the front row with a big smile across her face. She seemed very relieved, at ease, and happy.

The professor could hardly wait until the lecture period was over so he could ask Mary about her change in attitude from the evening before. When the class was dismissed, Mary hurried directly to the professor and explained what she had learned from her parents the night before.

Mary said she had called her mom and laid out the evidence she'd discovered in the lab concerning the blood types. Her mom, *(who was quite surprised to say the least!)*, quickly explained that since she and her husband weren't able to have children, they'd adopted Mary as a baby and that they hadn't ever gotten around to telling her. The parent child relationship was so lovingly strong and wonderful that the adoption had ceased to be on the minds of the parents and the daughter had no reason to suspect that she might have been adopted. Mary did have a younger sister, whom she knew was adopted because she was old enough to remember the event. But the wonderful family relationships gave Mary no reason to question whether or not *she* was adopted.

The absolute truth was present from the time Mary was adopted but she'd had no need to know the *complete* truth about her parentage until now. There was really no need for the complete revelation of the entire truth until Mary discovered something she couldn't explain or answer. There was never any selfish or self-protective motive involved. The absolute truth was given to her on a *need to know basis*.

It's through our study of God's marvelous creation and His continuing revelation to us of the principles of science that we learn more and more about Him and His wonderful creation. This discovery and learning process is forever ongoing. We can only imagine what He will reveal to us in the future when He knows the time is right and we have the *need to know* and the *ability to understand*.

Today's knowledge has increased so much that now many truths are being discovered that were impossible to comprehend in the past. Through DNA studies, convicted criminals have been found not guilty and freed from prison. Other crimes have been solved because of incriminating data obtained from increasingly sophisticated techniques. Family relationships have been proven or disproven through DNA findings. Analyses of chemical residues have answered many questions and on and on. The examples are seemingly endless.

These analyses are not subject to bias or prejudice, if they're done correctly. They only report the results of the tests, which must then be read and interpreted. They do not lie, but they can be misinterpreted. They tell us more of the truth about God's nature and creation when properly done and interpreted.

Going back to THE DELIMMA described in the PREFACE, the opposition between the three groups seems (at least to me) to have arisen primarily because of perceived differences in the knowledge and beliefs of the three groups.

The Bible Only Group and the Bible+Science Group believe in the inerrancy of the Bible as the true Word of God. The Science Only Group seems not to be concerned about Scripture, but only scientific knowledge.

As in the examples cited above, it's most important that God's account of His creation and the physical evidence left behind in the creative process reconcile themselves to each other. In so doing, they *reinforce each other for the ultimate truth.* One should not assume that the Biblical account is false, nor that the physical evidence of the creative process is false. *However, it is necessary to emphasize that it's always possible if not probable that either or both may be improperly interpreted at first.*

There *is* physical evidence left by the creative process that needs to be reconciled with the verbal testimony. *Both* the verbal testimony and physical evidence are true since both are testimony by the Trinity through word and deed. Let me emphasize that although both accounts are true, they are often misinterpreted by humankind. Any perceived discrepancies between the two accounts of creation (Biblical and scientific) are not in the account as given to us, but in our abilities to properly interpret them. Also, it is very probable that God has not yet chosen to reveal *all* His knowledge or information to us. Just like Johnny, humankind today still isn't yet ready to receive it and understand all of it.

We believe that God does not lie nor deliberately deceive us. Rather it's humankind that sometimes misinterprets the information He does give us. Is it conceivable that God would deliberately provide misinformation to us, in word or in deed, that would mislead us or give us conflicting information? Would He tell one story in one place and another story in another place? God would not tempt us or mislead us. *God does not lie*, therefore, we can believe everything He tells us both in Word and in deed. If we perceive any discrepancies, and since God has not lied or misled us, then *we* must have incorrectly interpreted some or part of His revelations. Also, we must remember that Satan is *always* there "stirring the pot" and trying to cause discord by pitting each group against the other two. We mustn't allow that to happen!

In the past, have we always properly interpreted His revelations? Are there examples where we improperly interpreted His revelations? Yes, there certainly are!

Some examples of previously misinterpreted revelations

The prime example.

This would be the fact that the Jewish people of the first century did not expect their savior to come as a helpless baby, but as a mighty king ready to assume a position of power and authority. They expected Him to rule and to restore Israel to the mighty earthly kingdom they had enjoyed during the reigns of David and Solomon.

Instead:

> He came to that which was his own, but his own did not receive him. (John 1:11 NIV)

It was the religious leaders of that day who most opposed to Him. They did not understand God's new plan for them or how He was going to accomplish it. The religious leaders of Jesus' day clung to their old, long held beliefs and caused His death at the hands of the Romans. It's very probable that they *really thought* they were doing God's will, but, sadly, they were wrong.

Another example is the belief that the earth is flat and not round.

The Bible speaks about the four corners of the earth twice in the book of Revelation:

> *After this I saw four angels standing at <u>the four corners</u> <u>of the earth</u>, holding back the four winds of the earth to prevent any wind from blowing on the land or on the sea or on any tree. (Rev 7:1 NIV)*

> *When the thousand years are over, Satan will be released from his prison and will go out to deceive the nations in <u>the four corners of the earth</u> — Gog and Magog — to gather them for battle. (Rev 20:7-8 NIV)*

For many centuries mankind interpreted the <u>four corners of the earth</u> as four individual points that define a flat surface, such as a tabletop. In Columbus' day and before, many believed that the earth was flat and that he, his ships, and all his crew would perish when they came to the edge of the earth and plunged into the deep abyss below. This belief still exists even today in people who call themselves the Flat Earth Society. They *know* from their interpretation of their Bible or other sources, that the earth indeed is flat and refuse to believe it's round in spite of the overwhelming evidence to the contrary. They hold tightly to their beliefs, ignoring the myriad of proofs of the earth being a sphere such as earth-orbiting spacecraft, round the world trips by thousands of people, views of the earth from the surface of the moon, etc.

Perhaps a better and more accurate interpretation of the *four corners of the earth* would to view them as the four points of the compass: North, South, East and West and that these directions had nothing to do with defining the earth as being flat. By taking this viewpoint, we find that there is no discrepancy between the Bible and scientific knowledge that the earth is a sphere. Instead, these findings of science actually help us to better interpret the Bible and thus strengthen our understanding of *both* the Bible and science.

Another example is in Psalms.

> *as far as the east is from the west, so far has he removed*
> *our transgressions from us. Ps 103:12 (NIV)*

Why would the author of Psalms use the directions east and west instead of north and south? How could he have known that if you went far enough north or south, you could only go the opposite direction when you reached either the north or south pole? Only by going either east or west, would you *never* stop going in that direction. But, humankind didn't know this until the second millennium AD. We now know that the earth has neither an east pole nor a west pole. Thus, the east or west direction of travel can't reverse. One could travel forever going either east or west and never reach the "end" of east or west. One would reach the end of a north direction of travel at the north pole and the end of a south direction of travel at the south pole. Therefore, north and south would *not* be good examples to express what God intended.

Did God inspire the author to use east and west to express how far He will separate us from our sins? Did the author know the endless extent of east and west as compared to the limited extent of north and south? Is this east-west choice of directions a simply a coincidence? I don't think so! Today, we know and understand more fully the wonderful meaning God intended, thanks to the *unity* of Scripture and the discoveries of science. How could those who lived in that period, and those who still believe the earth is flat, fully comprehend this wonderful teaching?

Another example is the belief that the earth is the center of the universe (geocentric) and that all other heavenly bodies revolve around it:

It was long believed that God would only create beings in His image and send His only Son for their salvation to a place that was the *center* of His creation and certainly not to a small planet orbiting a mediocre star in one of billions of other galaxies. The religious leaders of that time believed that teaching otherwise was heresy and should be punishable by death.

One such advocate opposing this long believed and accepted concept was Nicolaus Copernicus (1473–1543). He was a mathematician and astronomer who proposed that the sun was in a fixed position in the center and the earth revolved around it. This concept disturbed Aristotle's long held theory that all heavenly bodies moved in a uniform circular motion around the earth. After all, anyone should to be able to observe that the earth is stationary and that the sun rises in the east, moves up and over the surface of the earth and sinks slowly in the west. How could anyone be so stupid as to believe otherwise when the proof is right in front of you! All you have to do is open your eyes and observe the "facts."

At that time, Copernicus's heliocentric or sun-centred concept was very controversial. Nevertheless, it was the start of a change in the way the world was viewed, and Copernicus has come to be seen as the initiator of the Scientific Revolution.

About fifty years later in the early 1600's, there lived a man named Galileo Galilei. He was a religious man who agreed that the Bible could never be wrong. However, he said that the *interpreters* of the Bible could make mistakes and that it was a mistake to assume that the Bible had to be taken literally according to someone's *perceived infallible interpretation* of it.

Galileo made and used one of the first telescopes to study the heavenly bodies. He was the first to observe the mountains on the moon, the satellites of Jupiter, the rings of Saturn and the spots on the sun. His studies led him to support Copernicus's helicocentric theory and publish articles describing his findings and conclusions. He theorized that the earth orbited around the sun and rotated on its axis and that the earth was not fixed in position with all the other heavenly bodies revolving around it.

The religious leaders of that time used the following Scriptures as proof that the Bible clearly states that Galileo's theories were false:

Sun and moon stood still in the heavens. (Hab 3:11)

10

And

> *On the day the Lord gave the Amorites over to Israel, Joshua said to the Lord in the presence of Israel: "O sun, stand still over Gibeon, O moon, over the Valley of Aijalon." So the <u>sun stood still, and the moon stopped</u>, till the nation avenged itself on its enemies, as it is written in the Book of Jashar. The sun stopped in the middle of the sky and delayed going down about a full day. There has never been a day like it before or since, a day when the Lord listened to a man. Surely the Lord was fighting for Israel! (Josh 10:12-14 NIV)*

No doubt, these Scriptures accurately describe what the authors truly observed and concluded from their knowledge of astronomy and their own perception. We would've observed and recorded the same thing had we been there.

As Galileo's reputation grew it was met with a great deal of hatred and envy. He was finally denounced and turned over to the Inquisition for defending and developing the Copernican system. The Inquisition found the views of Copernicus and Galileo to be irreconcilable with the letter of the Scripture. Even though Galileo went to Rome to explain and defend himself, the religious leaders declared his theories to be absurd, false in philosophy, and contrary to the Holy Scriptures. While they were very learned in the scriptures, I wonder just how much *they* knew about the science of astronomy.

For most of the remainder of his life, Galileo was persecuted, prosecuted, and imprisoned for his research and what it revealed.

When Galileo was sixty-eight years old and ill, he was threatened with torture unless he publicly confessed that he had been wrong about the earth moving around the sun. He did confess, but at the end of his confession, he is reported to have said quietly, "And yet it moves."

The Church eventually lifted the ban on Galileo's Dialogue in 1822. By that time, it was common knowledge that the earth was not the center of the universe. Still later in the 1960's and 1970's, statements by the Vatican Council implied that Galileo was pardoned, and that he *had* suffered at the hands of the Church. Finally, in 1992, three years after Galileo Galilei's namesake satellite had been launched on its journey to Jupiter, the Vatican formally and publicly cleared Galileo of any wrongdoing. Yet, even today there are still some "geocentric" believers!

Another Example could be the interpretation of the word "day" in Genesis:

> *In the beginning God created the Heavens and the earth. (Gen 1:1 KJV)*
>
> *And God called the light **Day**, and the darkness he called Night. And the evening and the morning were the first **day**. (Gen 1:5 KJV)*
>
> *And the evening and the morning were the second **day**. (Gen 1:8 KJV)*
>
> *And the evening and the morning were the third **day** (Gen 1:13 KJV)*
>
> *And the evening and the morning were the fourth **day**. (Gen 1:19 KJV)*
>
> *And the evening and the morning were the fifth **day**. (Gen 1:23 KJV)*
>
> *And the evening and the morning were the sixth **day**. (Gen 1:31b KJV)*
>
> *And on the seventh <u>day</u> God ended his work which he had made; and he rested on the seventh **day** from all his work which he had made. (Gen 2:2 KJV)*

*These are the generations of the heavens and of the earth when they were created, in the **day** that the Lord God made the earth and the heavens. (Gen 2:4 KJV)*

In *every* instance cited above, the word day is translated from the Hebrew word *yowm* (yome) (Strong's Number 3117) which can be translated in various ways. But which of these meanings did God, through Moses, want to convey with the word *yowm*?

There are at least seven very interesting questions related to the above cited verses in Genesis if the word "day" as used there is believed to be a twenty-four hour period of time:

Question 1. If the first day lasted from the beginning to the end of the first day, just how long might that day have been?

*In the **beginning** God created the Heavens and the earth.*

And the earth was without form, and void; and darkness was upon the face of the deep. And the Spirit of God moved upon the face of the waters. And God said, Let there be light: and there was light. And God saw the light, that it was good: and God divided the light from the darkness.

*And God called the light **Day**, and the darkness he called Night. And the evening and the morning were the first **day**. (Gen 1:1-5 KJV)*

Question 2. Was the light part of the first day a 24 hour length of time?

*And God called the light **Day**, and the darkness he called Night. (Gen 1:5 KJV)*

Question 3. Regarding verses 14-19 - if the sun and moon weren't created until day four, what determined the length of days one, two, and three? Also, what was the planet earth doing from the beginning (Days one, two, and three) if the sun and moon were not yet "set in the firmament of the heaven" on Day four for it to revolve around?

*And God said, Let there be lights in the firmament of the heaven to divide the __day__ from the night; and let them be for signs, and for seasons, and for **days**, and years:*

And let them be for lights in the firmament of the heaven to give light upon the earth: and it was so.

*And God made two great lights; the greater light to rule the **day**, and the lesser light to rule the night: he made the stars also.*

And God set them in the firmament of the heaven to give light upon the earth,

*And to rule over the **day** and over the night, and to divide the light from the darkness: and God saw that it was good.*

*And the evening and the morning were the **fourth day**. (Gen 1:14-19 KJV)*

Question 4. If God created the green plants which require sunlight to live on day three, why did He wait until day 4 to create the sun to provide them with the life-sustaining light to allow photosynthesis to take place?

And God said, Let the earth bring forth grass, the herb yielding seed, and the fruit tree yielding fruit after his kind, whose seed is in itself, upon the earth: and it was so.

And the earth brought forth grass, and herb yielding seed after his kind, and the tree yielding fruit, whose seed was in itself, after his kind: and God saw that it was good.

*And the evening and the morning were the **third day**. (Gen 1:11-13 KJV)*

Question 5. If God began to rest from the wondrous process of His creation on day seven, and if we assume He is still resting from it and not creating anything else new, just how long has day seven been?

Thus the heavens and the earth were finished, and all the host of them.

*And on the seventh **day** God ended his work which he had made; and he rested on the seventh **day** from all his work which he had made.*

*And God blessed the seventh **day**, and sanctified it: because that in it he had rested from all his work which God created and made. (Gen 2:1-3 KJV)*

Question 6. Gen. 2:4 speaks of the day the Lord God made the earth and the heavens. How long was that day? Does it include days one through six?

*These are the generations of the heavens and of the earth when they were created, in the **day** that the Lord God made the earth and the heavens. (Gen 2:4 KJV)*

Question 7. Just what did <u>God</u> mean when He had Moses use the word "yowe" or "yome" for day in these Scriptures from Genesis?

To try to better understand and clarify the meaning of the word *day*, let's start with a **Hebrew Language Dictionary** definition: It will show that the word *day* can mean a twenty-four hour day or a much longer period of time:

> OT:3117 yowm (yome); from an unused root meaning to be hot; a day (as the warm hours), whether literal (from sunrise to sunset, or from one sunset to the next), or figurative (a space of time defined by an associated term), [often used adverb]:

> In the KJV the following translations of yowm have been used: - age, always, chronicals, continually (-ance), daily, ([birth-], each, to) day, (now a, two) days (agone), elder, end, evening, (for) ever (-lasting, -more), full, life, as (so) long as (... live), (even) now, old, outlived, perpetually, presently, remaineth, required, season, since, space, then, (process of) time, as at other times, in trouble, weather, (as) when, (a, the, within a) while (that), whole (+age), (full) year (-ly), younger.

> From Biblesoft's New Exhaustive Strong's Numbers and Concordance with Expanded Greek-Hebrew Dictionary. Copyright © 1994, 2003, 2006 Biblesoft, Inc. and International Bible Translators, Inc

If we consult several Bible dictionaries we find these definitions of *day:*

> Segment of time that includes the night (Gen 1:8) as in a twenty-four hour day. "Day" also stands in contrast to "night" (Num 11:32; Luke 18:7; Rev 7:15). The term may refer to an era (Matt 24:37) or to the span of human history (Gen 8:22), or specify a memorable event (Isa 9:4) or a significant time (Zeph 1:14-16). The term often has a metaphorical meaning. A "day" is important largely for what fills it rather than for its chronological dimension.

Evangelical Dictionary of Biblical Theology.
Copyright © 1996 by Baker Books. All rights reserved.
Used by permission.)

Another definition of day:

The Jews reckoned the day from sunset to sunset (Lev
23:32). It was originally divided into three parts (Ps
55:17). "The heat of the day" (1 Sam 11:11; Neh 7:3)
was at our nine o'clock, and "the cool of the day" just
before sunset (Gen 3:8). Before the Captivity the Jews
divided the night into three watches, (1) from sunset
to midnight (Lam 2:19); (2) from midnight till the cock-
crowing (Judg 7:19); and (3) from the cock-crowing till
sunrise (Ex 14:24). In the New Testament the division of
the Greeks and Romans into four watches was adopted
(Mark 13:35). (See WATCHES.)

The division of the day by hours is first mentioned in Dan
3:6,15; 4:19; 5:5. This mode of reckoning was borrowed
from the Chaldeans. The reckoning of twelve hours was
from sunrise to sunset, and accordingly the hours were
of variable length (John 11:9).

The word "day" sometimes signifies an indefinite time
(Gen 2:4; Isa 22:5; Heb 3:8, etc.). In Job 3:1 it denotes
a birthday, and in Isa 2:12; Acts 17:31, and 2 Tim 1:18,
the great day of final judgment.

Easton's Bible Dictionary, PC Study Bible formatted
electronic database Copyright © 2003, 2006 Biblesoft,
Inc. All rights reserved.)

Another definition of day:

This common word has caused some trouble to plain
readers, because they have not noticed that the word

is used in several different senses in the English Bible. When the different uses of the word are understood the difficulty of interpretation vanishes.

We note several different uses of the word:

It sometimes means the time from daylight till dark. This popular meaning is easily discovered by the context, The marked periods of this daytime were morning, noon and night, as with us. The early hours were sometimes called "the cool of the day" (Gen 3:8).

Day also means a period of 24 hours, or the time from sunset to sunset.

The word "day" is also used of an indefinite period, e.g. "the day" or "day that" means in general "that time" "day of trouble" "day of his wrath" "day of Yahweh" "day of the Lord" "day of salvation" "day of Jesus Christ".

It is used figuratively also in John 9:4, where "while it is day" means "while I have opportunity to work, as daytime is the time for work."

We must also bear in mind that with God time is not reckoned as with us (see Ps 90:4; 2 Peter 3:8).

On the meaning of "day" in the story of Creation we note (a) the word "day" is used of the whole period of creation (Gen 2:4); (b) these days are days of God, with whom one day is as a thousand years; the whole age or period of salvation is called "the day of salvation"; see above. So we believe that in harmony with Bible usage we may understand the creative days as creative periods.

International Standard Bible Encyclopaedia, Electronic Database Copyright © 1996, 2003, 2006 by Biblesoft, Inc. All rights reserved.)

Another definition of day:

The 24-hour period between two successive risings of the sun. The Hebrew people reckoned their day from evening to evening, the period of time between two successive sunsets (Gen 1:5,8; Ex 12:18; Lev 23:32).

The Bible also uses the word day in a symbolic sense, as in "the day of His wrath" (Job 20:28), and "the day of the Lord" (Isa 2:12; 13:6,9; Amos 5:18-20). The same phrase is used in the New Testament (1 Thess 5:2; 2 Peter 3:10), meaning "the day of the Lord Jesus" (1 Cor 5:5), or His second coming. To those who scoff at the delay of the Lord's return, Peter declared, "With the Lord one day is as a thousand years, and a thousand years as one day" (2 Peter 3:8). Also see TIME.

Nelson's Illustrated Bible Dictionary, Copyright © 1986, Thomas Nelson Publishers) defines DAY as follows:

Another definition of day:

The variable length of the natural day at different seasons led in the very earliest times to the adoption of the civil day (or one revolution of the sun) as a standard of time. The Hebrews reckoned the day from evening to evening, Lev 23:32, deriving it from Gen 1:5, "the evening and the morning were the first day." The Jews are supposed, like the modern Arabs, to have adopted from an early period minute specifications of the parts of the natural day. Roughly, indeed, they were content to divide it into "morning, evening and noonday," Ps

55:17, but when they wished for greater accuracy they pointed to six unequal parts, each of which was again subdivided. These are held to have been —

1. "the dawn."
2. "Sunrise."
3. "Heat of the day," about 9 o'clock.
4. "The two noons," Gen 43:16; Deut 28:29.
5. "The cool (lit. wind) of the day," before sunset, Gen 3:8 — so called by the Persians to this day.
6. "Evening." Before the captivity the Jews divided the night into three watches, Ps 63:6; 90:4, viz. the first watch, lasting till midnight, Lam 2:19, the "middle watch," lasting till cockcrow, Judg 7:19, and the "morning watch," lasting till sunrise. Ex 14:24. In the New Testament we have allusions to four watches, a division borrowed from the Greeks and Romans. These were —
7. From twilight till 9 o/clock, Mark 11:11; John 20:19.
8. Midnight, from 9 till 12 o'clock, Mark 13:35; 3 Macc 5:23.
9. Till daybreak. John 18:28. The word held to mean "hour" is first found in Dan 3:6,15; 5:5. Perhaps the Jews, like the Greeks, learned from the Babylonians the division of the day into twelve parts. In our Lord's time the division was common. John 11:9.

Smith's Bible Dictionary, PC Study Bible formatted electronic database Copyright © 2003, 2006 by Biblesoft, Inc. All rights reserved.) Gives the following definition:

But, *which* definition of day does God want us to use?

If we study Genesis 2:4 in context with Genesis Chapter 1, it is readily apparent that "the *day* that the Lord God made the earth and the heavens" couldn't have been a twenty-four hour day, but would've had to be at least six "days" long since Genesis 1 says six "days" were involved in God's creative process.

Since the Bible doesn't always explain all points of a given principle in one place, we study it in context with other scriptures as well. *Shouldn't we also examine the Scriptures in context with His revelations to us from the scientific study of His creation?* Wouldn't this method allow us to understand more fully the meaning God intended to give when we use His written revelation together with His revelations to us through the study of His science?

If we expand this method further, what does God tell us about the meaning of day from a study of His creation?

First of all, please bear with me through another parable.

Several years ago, a family was driving to their cabin in a remote mountainous region. Darkness was approaching on that cold winter evening and snow was beginning to fall, slowly at first, but becoming more and more intense with each mile they drove. It was a relatively short distance to the cabin and, under normal weather conditions, the trip could be made in about an hour. Tonight, however, it was a different story. The further they drove, the deeper the snow became and the driver drove slower and slower as he tried to keep the car on the slippery narrow winding road. He considered turning around and going back, but it seemed the better thing would be to continue on to their cabin, which could only be a short distance ahead.

After what seemed to be an eternity, the cabin came into view. The family got out of their car, hurriedly grabbed their suitcases, and ran into the cabin. It was dark and cold inside and there was no electricity. Most likely the power lines were down due to the heavy snow.

Everyone worked quickly, lighting candles, and building a fire in the fireplace. Soon a warm cozy atmosphere prevailed inside the cabin. Everyone was quite relieved to be safe after what seemed a very long and perilous journey. Then, someone posed the question, "I wonder what time it is?" No one seemed to know the answer.

As a result of rushing to make the trip, everyone who wore a wristwatch had overlooked winding his or her watch. (This was before the day of the auto-wind or battery powered watches.) The only clock in the cabin was a wind-up alarm clock. It had stopped and was useless to give the correct time. With no electricity, the TV or radio would not be used to give the time. No one wanted to go outside in the cold to use the car radio to determine the time. Surely there was an easier way to determine the time when they'd arrived at the cabin. The exact time of arrival wasn't critical, yet it was something to ponder. How could they determine the time they had arrived?

After several minutes of thought, one of the family members suggested, "Hey, let's wind the clock, set it at 12:00, and start it running. Then tomorrow, when we can determine the exact time of day, we can see how far that clock has run from 12:00. Then, if we subtract that time interval from the correct time, it'll tell us when we arrived here." Everyone agreed that it was a good idea.

The tired family wound and set the clock and went to bed. After a good night's sleep in warm beds, they awakened relaxed and refreshed the next morning. Shortly after they got up, they discovered that the power had been restored sometime during the night as they slept.

While they were preparing breakfast, they turned on the radio to get a weather forecast. The announcer mentioned that the current time was now 10:00 a.m. This reminded the family of the clock they set the night before. Quickly they looked at that clock and it read 8:00. This meant that they had set that clock 8 hours earlier than the present time of 10:00 a. m., or, at 2:00 a.m. That had to be the time they had arrived at the cabin. The question of when they arrived was now answered.

So, how does this story help us understand when the beginning was?

God's Clock

The Bible tells us

In the beginning, God created the heavens and the earth. (Gen 1:1 NIV)

But, when was the beginning? God may be trying to tell us by using a *type of clock* He started when He formed and molded the earth.

We know today that the center of the earth is very hot. It's so hot in fact that it's in a molten state as evidenced when volcanoes erupt and spew the molten lava out the top of their cone-shaped mountain that forms during the eruption process. While the molten lava cools, it hardens and becomes lava rock. While the newly formed earth cooled to form solid matter, some of the molten material formed crystalline structures. It's known that crystals form only when all the atoms or molecules are identical. One familiar example of this process is the formation of diamonds. In this instance, pure carbon atoms were heated to a very high temperature and placed under immense pressure. As they cooled, the carbon atoms joined together to form pure crystalline diamond rocks. We know that these rocks can be cut, ground, and polished to form the beautiful gems we know and treasure.

Another example of crystal formation is done repeatedly by some students for their science fair project. They make a very strong water solution of copper sulfate or other chemical and place it in a glass container. The water evaporates from the solution, causing the dissolved materials to precipitate out of solution and form beautiful blue crystals of pure copper sulfate. The crystals formed are very pure copper sulfate, even though other materials might be dissolved in the solution along with the copper sulfate. The crystals specifically exclude any other foreign material because they don't fit in the crystalline lattice structure of atoms of copper sulfate. Another example is that of rock candy made by causing sugar solutions to form pure sugar crystals sold as candy. This procedure is used in the chemical industry today to make very pure forms of certain chemicals.

Scientists have discovered that during the early days of the earth, uranium also formed crystalline structures as they cooled and hardened. They know that these crystals had to be composed of exactly the same molecules or atoms, or else the crystalline structure could not and would not form. Scientists also discovered that the form of uranium in these particular structures was the radioactive form of uranium and that the nuclei of the uranium atoms will break apart, or decay, *at a very slow but steady rate* over a very long period of time. This decay process emits radiations and changes the uranium atom into an atom of lead. These atoms of lead will still occupy the same space in the crystal where they existed as atoms of uranium when the crystal was originally formed.

Today, these crystals can be analyzed to determine how much of the original uranium has been changed into lead, and, knowing the *rate* of this change, determine how much *time* has passed since the crystal was originally formed. It's the same principle used in starting the clock in the cabin. By determining how long the clock had run, the family was able to determine when they arrived at the cabin and started the clock. By analyzing this uranium clock today, it is possible to determine when it was started, that is, when the crystal of uranium was formed.

The data from these measurements consistently indicate that these uranium/lead crystals were formed about 4.5 billion years ago.

Are these crystals a result of the creation process or something put here on earth by Satan to try to confuse us and destroy our faith? Or, is God trying to reveal Himself and His creative process to us more completely through man's study of His natural world and tell us what He meant by the word day? Were the people of Moses' time capable of understanding billions of years?

If the beginning was at least 4.5 billion years ago, then how long might each day have been? Was it twenty-four hours, or a longer period of time? Both of these definitions are given for the word day. Which does God intend for us to use here? Which of these does He intend for us to use now--today? Shouldn't we interpret the meaning of the word day in context with what God is revealing to us through the study of His marvelous creation?

The Geologic Time Chart.

The Geologic Time Chart was made by scientists in an attempt to organize, in an orderly fashion, the things they've discovered through their research in geology, astronomy, paleontology, archaeology, biology, and a portion of almost every other scientific discipline. It's the combined and cooperative efforts of thousands of individuals to put together the pieces of their discoveries (God's revelations to them) into a unified description of the universe from its origin to today. It seems to concentrate primarily on the fossil records laid down in strata of rock in the earth that tell a story of the order of appearance of the myriads of plant and animal life forms. Through careful analysis and comparison, time lines can be established. The Geologic Time Chart is constantly under close scrutiny for errors and omissions by thousands of scientists whose main goal is to continually revise it, improve it, and correct any errors.

The main thing it shows is that some primitive life forms present in earlier times are not alive today, and the more advanced life forms alive today were absent in the earlier times. It shows an ordered progression of appearance of life from the simpler forms to the more complex forms. It's very interesting to note that a similar order of appearance is described in Genesis, but with only a small amount of detail given. As with Johnny in the Introduction, God gave just enough detail to the people in that day and time to explain in simple terms that He made everything including humans. Today, God is telling us the same story, except that now He is including a much greater degree of explanation and detail because we are better able to understand His revelations through the scientific study of His creation.

As one who's been fortunate enough to study some of the details of this aspect of science, it has revealed to me a most beautiful and wonderful story of the orderly progression of life forms from the lower to the higher. This process is so intertwined between all forms of life, weather patterns, geologic events (volcanoes, meteor impacts on earth), changes in the earth's atmosphere, and on and on that it remarkably demonstrates the immense power and intelligence of God. It begins to explain the order of the creation and the forces involved. However, it does not yet explain completely the mechanisms--exactly how He did it all-- from the smallest subatomic particle to the vastness of outer space.

The Immense Size Of the Universe.

Scientists can measure the distances from the earth to the billions and billions of other objects present in our universe. For example, we know that the moon is just over 200,000 miles from earth and the sun is ninety-three million miles away from us. We know that light from the sun travels at 186,000 miles per second and that it takes over eight minutes for light leaving the surface of the sun to reach the earth.

The increase in accuracy of measuring distances to very remote galaxies requires the use of units of measurement much greater than miles. A comparison would be to try to measure the distance from Los Angeles to New York City in inches instead of miles. The number of inches would be too great to comprehend easily. The same is true in the measurement of distances in the universe. Thus, scientists have adopted a measurement called the light year. A light year is defined as the distance light would travel in the period of one year. A light year would be equal to the distance obtained by multiplying 186,000 miles per second times 60 seconds/minute times 60 minutes per hour times 24 hours per day times 365 days per year.

Or: 186,000 x 60 x 60 x 24 x 365 = 5,865,696,000,000 miles.

(Actually the number is slightly larger since there are just over 365 days in a year--thus requiring the "leap year" of 366 days every fourth year.)

Even using light years to measure distances in outer space, it requires millions and even billions of light years to express the distances from the earth to the most distant objects in our universe. *This means that light from those objects left them whatever million or billion light years they are away and it's just now reaching earth so we can observe that light and the images it brings to us.* Just consider that these images show the condition of the object as it appeared when the light left that particular object. It doesn't give us any information about what that object looks like today, or even if it still exists.

These scientific discoveries indicate that the beginning had to be at least several billions of years ago since it took light that long to arrive here on earth. More importantly, this information comes from our study of God's universe. Is God trying to confuse or mislead us with these findings? Or, could it be something that Satan has put there just to confuse and mislead us? If that's true, then the Genesis account would have to be wrong, because Satan, and not God, would have been the Creator. As sly and wicked and powerful as Satan may be, does he have the intelligence or power to create anything greater than sin? And we know that a just and loving God would not be untruthful to His children whom he loves dearly in spite of their sins.

God's testimony is always true whether it's from His verbal testimony or from the physical evidence He has left for us to study, to properly interpret, and to better understand Him.

Can we, and should we, use *all* of God's revelations to us so that we can more completely understand Him?

Note: The following material is taken from various authors of religious literature and is *not* the product of this author.

No honest criticism can destroy God's truth. A study of nature does not banish God or His design from nature. If God created all things, then all things are under His government. Then the earth may be studied religiously. Then it is reasonable that He should take an interest in nature.

What we learn here about God from the study of His creation: --

1. *His being.*
2. *His eternity.*
3. *His omnipotence.*
4. *His absolute freedom.*
5. *His infinite wisdom.*
6. *His essential goodness.*

Paraphrased from (J. White.)

(from The Biblical Illustrator Copyright © 2002, 2003, 2006 Ages Software, Inc. and Biblesoft, Inc.)

Another citation:

Things to be awaited

V. WE WAIT FOR THE <u>MYSTERY</u> TO BE TAKEN OFF FROM LIFE. The crucial test of a thoughtful mind is a sense of the mystery of life in this world. This highest order of mind is not antagonistic to faith; it is simply conscious of the incomprehensible range of truth. None but an inferior mind has a plan of the universe; it is to the thoughtless that all things are plain. What is life? What is matter? What is the relation between them? What is creation? Granting evolution, what started the evolving process? Assuming God, what is the relation of creation to Him? What the relation of man? What is this that thinks and wills and loves -- this I? And then, *what is it all for? Is there a final purpose and an order tending to it, or is it but the whirl of molecules, the dust of the universe circling for a moment in space, of which we are but some atoms? Is there a bridge between consciousness and the external world, or a gulf that cannot be spanned or fathomed? Is life a reality, or is it a dream from which we may awake in some world of reality to find that this world was but the vision of a night? It is useless to deny that this mystery carries with it a sense of pain.*

(from The Biblical Illustrator Copyright © 2002, 2003, 2006 Ages Software, Inc. and Biblesoft, Inc.)

Another citation:

III. Evolution and Man

The conclusion from the whole is, that, up to the present hour, science and the Biblical views of God, man, and the world, do not stand in any real relation of conflict. Each book of God's writing reflects light upon the pages of the other, but neither contradicts the other's essential testimony. Science itself seems now disposed to take a less materialistic view of the origin and nature of things than it did a decade or two ago, and to interpret the creation more in the light of the spiritual. The experience of the Christian believer, with the work of missions in pagan lands, furnishes a testimony that cannot be disregarded to the reality of this spiritual world, and of the regenerating, transforming forces proceeding from it. To God be all the glory!

(from The Fundamentals: A Testimony to the Truth, Electronic Database. Copyright © 1997, 2003, 2005, 2006 by Biblesoft, Inc.)

Another citation:

> *Comments on Job 14:4 -- "A Clean Thing Out Of An Unclean."*
>
> I. *EVOLUTION. We are not now concerned with the scientific aspect of the question of evolution. That must be determined by the men of science. But there is a religious aspect of it that calls for attention, because some are dismayed as though evolution had banished God from his universe. Now, if this idea of the world is set forth as a substitute for the theological conception of creation and providence, it is removed from its rightful sphere and made to trespass on a foreign domain, where it cannot justify the claims of its supporters. There it is confronted by Job's question, "Who can bring a clean thing out of an unclean?" Evolution signifies a certain kind of progress. But the cause must be equal to the effect. It is contrary to the very law of causation that dead matter should produce life, and that the merely animal should produce the spiritual human being. For every elevation and addition a corresponding cause is needed. If the unclean ape were the ancestor of a saint, something must have been added that was not in the ape. Whence was this? It must have had a cause. Thus we may see that evolution requires the idea of the Divine, not only at the primal creation, but throughout the process.*
>
> *(from The Pulpit Commentary, Electronic Database. Copyright © 2001, 2003, 2005, 2006 by Biblesoft, Inc. All rights reserved.)*

These preceding excerpts of scholarly material by several authors has been included here to try to show that the Bible *versus* Science mind-set so prevalent for the past few centuries, is slowly but surely being modified into a *unity* of Bible *and* Science understanding and perspective.

In the first century the religious leaders held strongly to their long established beliefs and interpretations they'd become so comfortable believing. They couldn't, and wouldn't, accept the new teachings of Jesus because they conflicted with what *they* believed and interpreted from the Old Testament Scriptures. They felt that Jesus' teachings were so different they had to be rejected and could never be considered as a fulfillment of the many prophecies of His coming found in their Hebrew Scriptures. As Christians today, we know that Jesus was the long-promised King of Kings who came at the Father's desire to save us from the sins we all commit. Sadly, the religious leaders then couldn't, or wouldn't, accept His new teachings.

Today, it seems to me, that we're being given new teachings via completely different means. Millions of individuals are studying the marvels and mysteries of God's wonderful creation, discovering that some of these findings are different from the Genesis account of creation that we've understood, believed, and taught for so long. Just as with Johnny in the earlier parable, God told us in Genesis, "I made you," because that's all we could understand at that point of development of humankind. Today, we *can* begin to understand more completely how He created everything and, now, He is revealing these things to us through our study of His creation. These new revelations are from God just as much as are the Scriptures He has given us. They shouldn't be mutually exclusive, but complementary to each other to the extent that we can use each revelation to help explain the other. As previously stated, God does not lie to us or mislead us. He does, however, expect us to do the following:

> *Do your best to present yourself to God as one approved,*
> *a workman who does not need to be ashamed and who*
> *correctly handles the word of truth. (2 Tim 2:15 NIV)*

If we can understand that everything God does or says is the Word of truth, then we're charged with properly studying, interpreting, and reconciling everything He has given us and is giving us through the Bible and science. If we do this, won't it help us to better understand Him and His might, power, knowledge, love and purpose for each of us?

Yet there are, and will probably be, those individuals who won't swerve from their beliefs just as many in Jesus' time held to their beliefs. Perhaps we should examine and re-examine our beliefs frequently to make sure that *we're* holding fast to what *God wants* us to believe and not what *we want* to believe about Him. If we actively seek God's will in our lives from every true source available to us, how can it do anything but strengthen our faith and our resolve to do His will?

Yet, in spite of all the evidence science tells us, some still argue, "Couldn't God have done all this in six, twenty-four hour days?" Almost every Bible believing individual will agree that He *could* have done it that way, if that had been His plan. Then the individual asking this question will smile in agreement and conclude that the problem is solved, and the case is closed, He *did* do it in six, twenty-four hour days. Now, let's move forward. But, couldn't God have done it in much longer periods of time? This answer also has to be yes as well.

What does God's physical evidence teach us as compared to how some interpret the word day in Genesis? Can it be reconciled with the account in the Bible? Yes, it certainly can, *if* we use the Bible *and* the findings revealed in the study of science *together.* After all, which is stronger—each of God's accounts viewed by itself, or a compilation of all of His truths with each truth being used to understand and clarify the other?

We can see from God's testimony to us (Biblical as well scientific) that He is the most powerful, important, and loving being in the entire universe.

And, *one thing is for sure.* We'd certainly better pay attention to *everything* He is telling us and try our best to understand as completely and accurately as possible what we should know and understand from these revelations and what they require us to do.

Hopefully, our faith will be greatly strengthened as a result, so that we can glorify God all the more by loving Him and obeying His commands to us. This is certainly the case with me, and I fervently hope and pray that the same will be true for the reader as well.

Perhaps this is the best explanation of the main thing I'm trying to accomplish by writing this book!

CHAPTER 2

How God Reveals Himself to Us

If we look at the history of humankind since the beginning, we see that God has revealed Himself to us in various ways and to varying degrees over time by using various covenants between God and humankind.

> *In the past God spoke to our forefathers through the prophets <u>at many times and in various ways</u>, but in these last days he has spoken to us by his Son, whom he appointed heir of all things, and <u>through whom he made the universe</u>. The Son is the radiance of God's glory and the exact representation of his being, sustaining all things by his powerful word. After he had provided purification for sins, he sat down at the right hand of the Majesty in heaven. So he became as much superior to the angels as the name he has inherited is superior to theirs.* (Heb 1:1-4 *NIV*)

In the Bible we read about God's revelations to us using the various covenants He made with His children, first with Adam, through many individuals, then to Jesus Christ. The following are some of the **covenants** God made with various individuals and groups of people.

God's Covenant with Adam:

> *The Lord God took the man and put him in the Garden*
> *of Eden to work it and, take care of it. And the Lord God*
> *commanded the man, "You are free to eat from any tree*
> *in the garden; but you must not eat from the tree of the*
> *knowledge of good and evil, for when you eat of it you*
> *will surely die." (Gen 2:15-17 NIV)*

Here God made a **covenant** with Adam with just *two conditions*:

(1) To live in the Garden of Eden and to take care of it, and,
(2) Not to eat from the Tree of the Knowledge of Good
     and Evil.

God saw that Adam was alone and lonely, so He made Eve to be his wife and companion. Together they must've had a wonderfully close relationship with God until they broke God's **covenant** with them after they ate from the forbidden tree.

> *Then the man and his wife heard the sound of the Lord*
> *God as he was walking in the garden in the cool of the*
> *day, and they hid from the Lord God among the trees of*
> *the garden. But the Lord God called to the man, "Where*
> *are you?" He answered, "I heard you in the garden,*
> *and I was afraid because I was naked; so I hid." (Gen*
> *3:8-10 NIV)*

What could be more wonderful than Adam and Eve's close relationship of walking and talking with the Lord God in the Garden of Eden in the cool of the day? What a terrible thing to lose because of their disobedience and sin. As a result, God expelled them from the garden and placed heavy burdens on them and their descendants, even reaching to us today.

God's Covenant with Noah:

As the human population of the earth increased in numbers, God observed that:

> *The Lord saw how great man's wickedness on the earth had become, and that every inclination of the thoughts of his heart was only evil all the time. The Lord was grieved that he had made man on the earth, and his heart was filled with pain. So the Lord said, "I will wipe mankind, whom I have created, from the face of the earth — men and animals, and creatures that move along the ground, and birds of the air — for I am grieved that I have made them." But Noah found favor in the eyes of the Lord.*
>
> *This is the account of Noah.*
>
> *Noah was a righteous man, blameless among the people of his time, and he walked with God. Noah had three sons: Shem, Ham and Japheth.*
>
> *Now the earth was corrupt in God's sight and was full of violence. God saw how corrupt the earth had become, for all the people on earth had corrupted their ways. So God said to Noah, "I am going to put an end to all people, for the earth is filled with violence because of them. I am surely going to destroy both them and the earth. (Gen 6:5-14 NIV)*

So-- God had Noah and his sons build an ark to save themselves and selected life forms from drowning in the flood that would follow. After the flood had come and the waters had receded, God made another **covenant** with humankind:

> *Then God said to Noah and to his sons with him: "I now establish my **covenant** with you and with your*

descendants after you and with every living creature that was with you — the birds, the livestock and all the wild animals, all those that came out of the ark with you — every living creature on earth. I establish my **covenant** *with you: Never again will all life be cut off by the waters of a flood; never again will there be a flood to destroy the earth." (Gen 9:8-11 NIV)*

God's Covenant with Abraham:

"When Abram was ninety-nine years old, the Lord appeared to him and said, "I am God Almighty; walk before me and be blameless. I will confirm my **covenant** *between me and you and will greatly increase your numbers."*

Abram fell facedown, and God said to him, "As for me, this is my **covenant** *with you: You will be the father of many nations. No longer will you be called Abram; your name will be Abraham, for I have made you a father of many nations. I will make you very fruitful; I will make nations of you, and kings will come from you. I will establish my* **covenant** *as an everlasting* **covenant** *between me and you and your descendants after you for the generations to come, to be your God and the God of your descendants after you. The whole land of Canaan, where you are now an alien, I will give as an everlasting possession to you and your descendants after you; and I will be their God."*

Then God said to Abraham, "As for you, you must keep my **covenant**, *you and your descendants after you for the generations to come. This is my* **covenant** *with you and your descendants after you, the* **covenant** *you are to keep: Every male among you shall be circumcised. You are to undergo circumcision, and it will be the sign of the* **covenant** *between me and you. For the* *generations to come every male among you who is eight days old must be circumcised, including those born in your household or bought with money from a foreigner — those who are not your offspring. Whether born in your household or bought with your money, they must be circumcised. My **covenant** in your flesh is to be an everlasting **covenant**. Any uncircumcised male, who has not been circumcised in the flesh, will be cut off from his people; he has broken my **covenant**." (Gen 17:1-14 NIV)*

God's Covenant of the Priesthood

*The Lord said to Moses, "Phinehas son of Eleazar, the son of Aaron, the priest, has turned my anger away from the Israelites; for he was as zealous as I am for my honor among them, so that in my zeal I did not put an end to them. Therefore tell him I am making my **covenant** of peace with him. He and his descendants will have a **covenant** of a lasting priesthood, because he was zealous for the honor of his God and made atonement for the Israelites." (Num 25:10-13 NIV)*

*Remember them, O my God, because they defiled the priestly office and the **covenant** of the priesthood and of the Levites. (Neh 13:29 NIV)*

God's Covenant of Sinai

*Then the Lord said to Moses, "Write down these words, for in accordance with these words I have made a **covenant** with you and with Israel." Moses was there with the Lord forty days and forty nights without eating bread or drinking water. And he wrote on the tablets the words of the **covenant**—the Ten Commandments. (Ex 34:27-28 NIV)*

Practically the entire book of Leviticus expands on the Old Testament **covenant** the Lord God gave to Moses. These laws were to govern the Jewish people beyond what was given in the Ten Commandments.

> ***Lev 26:3-46*** *"'If you follow my decrees and are careful to obey my commands, I will send you rain in its season, and the ground will yield its crops and the trees of the field their fruit. Your threshing will continue until grape harvest and the grape harvest will continue until planting, and you will eat all the food you want and live in safety in your land.*
>
> *"'I will grant peace in the land, and you will lie down and no one will make you afraid. I will remove savage beasts from the land, and the sword will not pass through your country. You will pursue your enemies, and they will fall by the sword before you. Five of you will chase a hundred, and a hundred of you will chase ten thousand, and your enemies will fall by the sword before you.*
>
> *"'I will look on you with favor and make you fruitful and increase your numbers, and I will keep my **covenant** with you. You will still be eating last year's harvest when you will have to move it out to make room for the new. I will put my dwelling place among you, and I will not abhor you. I will walk among you and be your God, and you will be my people. I am the Lord your God, who brought you out of Egypt so that you would no longer be slaves to the Egyptians; I broke the bars of your yoke and enabled you to walk with heads held high.*
>
> *"'But if you will not listen to me and carry out all these commands, and if you reject my decrees and abhor my laws and fail to carry out all my commands and so violate my **covenant**, then I will do this to you: I will bring upon you sudden terror, wasting diseases and fever that*

will destroy your sight and drain away your life. You will plant seed in vain, because your enemies will eat it. I will set my face against you so that you will be defeated by your enemies; those who hate you will rule over you, and you will flee even when no one is pursuing you.

"'If after all this you will not listen to me, I will punish you for your sins seven times over. I will break down your stubborn pride and make the sky above you like iron and the ground beneath you like bronze. Your strength will be spent in vain, because your soil will not yield its crops, nor will the trees of the land yield their fruit.

"'If you remain hostile toward me and refuse to listen to me, I will multiply your afflictions seven times over, as your sins deserve. I will send wild animals against you, and they will rob you of your children, destroy your cattle and make you so few in number that your roads will be deserted.

*"'If in spite of these things you do not accept my correction but continue to be hostile toward me, I myself will be hostile toward you and will afflict you for your sins seven times over. And I will bring the sword upon you to avenge the breaking of the **covenant**. When you withdraw into your cities, I will send a plague among you, and you will be given into enemy hands. When I cut off your supply of bread, ten women will be able to bake your bread in one oven, and they will dole out the bread by weight. You will eat, but you will not be satisfied.*

"'If in spite of this you still do not listen to me but continue to be hostile toward me, then in my anger I will be hostile toward you, and I myself will punish you for your sins seven times over. You will eat the flesh of your sons and the flesh of your daughters. I will destroy your high places, cut down your incense altars and pile

your dead bodies on the lifeless forms of your idols, and I will abhor you. I will turn your cities into ruins and lay waste your sanctuaries, and I will take no delight in the pleasing aroma of your offerings. I will lay waste the land, so that your enemies who live there will be appalled. I will scatter you among the nations and will draw out my sword and pursue you. Your land will be laid waste, and your cities will lie in ruins. Then the land will enjoy its sabbath years all the time that it lies desolate and you are in the country of your enemies; then the land will rest and enjoy its sabbaths. All the time that it lies desolate, the land will have the rest it did not have during the Sabbaths you lived in it.

"'As for those of you who are left, I will make their hearts so fearful in the lands of their enemies that the sound of a windblown leaf will put them to flight. They will run as though fleeing from the sword, and they will fall, even though no one is pursuing them. They will stumble over one another as though fleeing from the sword, even though no one is pursuing them. So you will not be able to stand before your enemies. You will perish among the nations; the land of your enemies will devour you. Those of you who are left will waste away in the lands of their enemies because of their sins; also because of their fathers' sins they will waste away.

*"'But if they will confess their sins and the sins of their fathers — their treachery against me and their hostility toward me, which made me hostile toward them so that I sent them into the land of their enemies — then when their uncircumcised hearts are humbled and they pay for their sin, I will remember my **covenant** with Jacob and my **covenant** with Isaac and my **covenant** with Abraham, and I will remember the land. For the land will be deserted by them and will enjoy its Sabbaths while it lies desolate without them. They will pay for their*

*sins because they rejected my laws and abhorred my decrees. Yet in spite of this, when they are in the land of their enemies, I will not reject them or abhor them so as to destroy them completely, breaking my **covenant** with them. I am the Lord their God. But for their sake I will remember the **covenant** with their ancestors whom I brought out of Egypt in the sight of the nations to be their God. I am the Lord.'"*

These are the decrees, the laws and the regulations that the Lord established on Mount Sinai between himself and the Israelites through Moses. (Lev 26:3-46 NIV)

God's New Covenant

In God's time and in God's way, He further revealed Himself and more of His divine plan for humankind through His Son, many times referred to in the Scriptures as the *Mystery of God.*

*But the ministry Jesus has received is as superior to theirs as the **covenant** of which he is mediator is superior to the old one, and it is founded on better promises.*

*For if there had been nothing wrong with that first **covenant**, no place would have been sought for another. But God found fault with the people and said:*

*"The time is coming, declares the Lord, when I will make a new **covenant** with the house of Israel and with the house of Judah. It will not be like the **covenant** I made with their fore fathers when I took them by the hand to lead them out of Egypt, because they did not remain faithful to my **covenant**, and I turned away from them, declares the Lord.*

> *This is the **covenant** I will make with the house of Israel after that time, declares the Lord. I will put my laws in their minds and write them on their hearts. I will be their God, and they will be my people. No longer will a man teach his neighbor, or a man his brother, saying, 'Know the Lord, 'because they will all know me, from the least of them to the greatest. For I will forgive their wickedness and will remember their sins no more."*
>
> *By calling this **covenant** "new," he has made the first one obsolete; and what is obsolete and aging will soon disappear. (Heb 8:6-13 NIV)*

It would seem obvious from the above-cited examples that God does things in His own way and in His own time. It would be very doubtful that any believer would completely understand His reasons for doing the things He did or the order in which He did them. Jehovah God is all-knowing and all-powerful. Probably His reasons for doing what He does, when He does them, and why He does them aren't comprehensible to the mere humans that we are.

One thing most believers can agree upon is that God does things when humankind is best ready to accept them and in need of receiving them. For example, He did not send Christ to Adam and Eve. He did not send Christ to Sinai, He sent Moses instead. He waited many years to send the Savior when the time was right. The Bible abounds with similar examples of His doing things when it was best for His creation.

God's past dealings with His creation are a matter of record. We know that humankind's abilities and knowledge are growing today as never before and at an ever increasing rate. *Is God finished revealing Himself to us?* If not, then how and when might He further reveal Himself to us? What new revelations is humankind now ready to receive? What new revelations has He already given us that we've yet to recognize? Perhaps now we are like Mary in Chapter 1 who needed more information to explain why her blood type was not the same as her parents. We're now in need of more information from

God to help us understand Him better and to answer new questions we're discovering through our studies of God's Word (the Bible—His book) and God's work (His creation--His deeds).

God's New Covenant -- Continued?

In the past, whenever humankind needed new input from God, He was there to reveal His progressive divine plan for the benefit of His children. Our New Testament was written in the first century AD, with the last book, Revelation, believed to have been written about AD 90 to AD 95. Have we had any new revelations from Him since that time? Most authorities, who've studied when the various books of the Bible were written, agree that the longest silent period in the Bible is that interval between the last of the Old Testament and the first of the New Testament. This is believed to be a period of time of about 400 years. Has God now been silent in His communication with His children for almost 2,000 years? That's *five times longer* than the earlier silent period!

Or, perhaps we've been given new revelations but we just haven't recognized them --*yet.*

> The **heavens** declare the glory of God; and the **firmament** showeth His handiwork. *(Ps 19:1 KJV)*

It seems that the intent of this Scripture is to show the power and majesty of the Creator through the examination of His universe. We can most certainly see that the heavens and earth are very immense and complex, just through a casual observation of them.

No one can deny the orderliness, regularity, and complexity of the universe and God's laws of science that make it possible for them to exist and to continue to function since the beginning of time.

In this Scripture, is God suggesting, or even commanding, that we study, and continue to study, all of His creation in order to see and understand His mighty power and infinite wisdom and planning? If He wants us to study His creation, then one might ask, *to what extent* should we examine and study it? Through casual observation or through the use of today's very advanced analytical devices, we can learn greater and deeper detail of His creation. God isn't through with us yet. He has much, much more to reveal to us.

The Heavens: (There are many definitions of heaven(s), but for this discussion I would like to restrict the definition to include everything in the universe except the planet earth.)

To what extent is it acceptable and correct to observe the heavens? With an optical telescope? How about a radio telescope? How about using a spectrometer to measure the wavelengths of light coming from the far reaches of outer space to enable us to determine the chemical composition of the matter emitting that light? Should we use radar and lasers to measure distances from earth to the moon, from earth to the sun, or from earth to other objects in our solar system? Should we try to measure distances to the more distant objects of the universe? Just how far does the universe extend? What's beyond the known universe? How far does space extend? The questions are "astronomical" in number and complexity.

There's so much knowledge available today that no one person can even begin to comprehend even a portion of an infinitely small part of it. It's been said, facetiously of course, that a scientist doing greater and deeper studies into his area of interest learns more and more about less and less until he or she knows everything about nothing. Yet, we know that *God does know everything* from the largest entity down to the smallest particle. And, what's more, *He made it all and keeps everything working.*

> *Everything we do know or ever will know about the heavens certainly does show the glory of God*

The Firmament: (There are many definitions of firmament, but for this discussion I'd like to restrict the definition to planet earth.)

To what extent, then, is it acceptable to examine the *firmament*? It would include the study of the planet itself, its interior, its mountains, valleys, oceans, lakes, glaciers, climate, as well as all the present and past life forms. These are just some of the main divisions, with each division possessing infinitely numerous subdivisions. In every aspect of these studies, we see God's hands at work and discover the very ordered process by which the creation was accomplished through the evidence He left behind for us. This is something that earlier humans couldn't understand. God is revealing to us the things He would have us know because *now* we can begin to know and comprehend them.

A study of the firmament *certainly does show God's handiwork.*

Everything we discover and learn through the study of God's creation are the "footprints" and "fingerprints" He left during the creation process. Are they not just as true and real as the inspired words He gave to the many authors of the books of the Bible? Paul told Timothy (and us) to "study and rightly interpret the word of truth". Is this "word of truth" restricted just to the Bible, or does it include everything He has revealed, and will reveal, to us through a careful study of the physical evidence left by His process of creation? Shouldn't we study *everything* God has revealed to us? All of God's words and deeds are true. But, we must correctly interpret them (a very difficult and a continually ongoing process) if we are to know and understand God's truth.

Since we know that all of God's revelations to us are true, shouldn't we use and study them to get the clearest possible understanding of His plan for us? Granted, sometimes we've misinterpreted some of the Scripture, and sometimes we've misinterpreted the findings of science, but that's *our* problem and not God's. It is *our* responsibility to "study and rightly interpret" the "word of truth". We can't achieve this if we ignore either the study of the Bible or the study of God's creation.

Just like Johnny as he grew older, we are becoming increasingly able to comprehend and appreciate what God is revealing to us now in accordance with His will.

As new scientific methods are developed and perfected, we will continue to discover more and more about Him and His creation. He will not reveal anything to us that's contrary to His will or is untrue, unless we mistakenly, and sometimes even purposely, misinterpret His revelations to us. We need to seek after, and be ever alert, to His revelations to us and make sure that we interpret them correctly. We must be very careful not to pick and choose only those findings that support our beliefs and ignore those that don't. We can, and should, use *all* of His revelations to us to see more of His true picture. We're always learning new things every day, both in the study of the Bible and in the study of science.

At this point we need to remember that Christ's coming was prophesied early in Genesis, repeatedly mentioned in the Old Testament, and finally revealed when He was born in Bethlehem and began his life and teaching and preaching. Just imagine the new things God may reveal to us in the future. Could this be part of **God's new covenant -- continued**?

If these revelations are not part of His plan, then what are they? Please consider the following:

*Heaven and earth will pass away, but my **words** will never pass away. (Matt 24:35 NIV)*

*Heaven and earth will pass away, but my **words** will never pass away. (Mark 13:31 NIV)*

*Heaven and earth will pass away, but my **words** will never pass away. (Luke 21:33 NIV)*

It is obvious here that Jesus' *words* include everything he *said* that is recorded in our Bible. Is it also possible, or even probable that it includes what he *did* in the creative process?

Through him all things were made; without him nothing was made that has been made. (John 1:3 NIV)

Consider also:

> *For if their purpose or activity is of human origin, it will*
> *fail. But if it is from God, you will not be able to stop*
> *these men; you will only find yourselves fighting against*
> *God. (Acts 5:38a-39 NIV)*

Is our study of God's science an activity of human origin that will fail, or is it something from God that He wants us to do that He will not allow to fail? And, what is this about *fighting against God*? Is it possible to fight against God today?

This Scripture should apply to us today as well as to those when it was written, and it should apply both to the study of the Bible and the study of science.

CHAPTER 3

God's Mystery

God's Revelations to Us in His Way and in His Time

As stated earlier, most, if not all, believers in the Judeo-Christian God will probably agree that God does things in His way and in His time. Even atheists and agnostics marvel at the complexity and orderliness of the universe, from the most distant galaxies down to the smallest subatomic particles, and everything in between these two extremes. Yet, they give no credit to God for its existence.

We know from Scripture that Adam and Eve were expelled from the Garden of Eden because of their sin. They were removed from a paradise situation to be on their own. Humankind remained in this sinful condition until they were redeemed by Jesus' death on the cross allowing them to be forgiven of their sins and to receive the gift of everlasting life in heaven.

One might ask why Jesus didn't come to earth when Adam and Eve sinned in the Garden of Eden. Or, why didn't He come during the time of Noah to save all those who drowned in the flood? Or, why didn't he come when Moses received the Ten Commandments on Mount Sinai? Why did God wait thousands of years to send His Son for the salvation of humankind?

The only answer that can be given is that God does things His own way and in His own time. Only He knows what is best and when is best. It is something we don't and can't know or understand.

Referring back to the story about Johnny's question and his Dad's answer, perhaps there is a parallel relationship here. God, our Father, will give us answers when He knows we can best understand them.

God was not ready to reveal Himself and His plan to humankind earlier, not because He couldn't, but because He knew humankind was not yet ready to receive it or understand it. It is, and has been, a *mystery* to humankind hidden for long ages past.

This word *mystery* occurs many times in the Bible and has been defined repeatedly in biblical literature. Some of these definitions of *mystery* as used in the Bible are as follows:

Nelson's Bible Dictionary, defines *mystery* as "The hidden, eternal plan of God that *is being revealed* to God's people in accordance with his plan."

New Unger's Bible Dictionary, defines *mystery* as "...the plan of God *hitherto unrevealed*...but one that contains a supernatural element that still remains in spite of the revelation."

Both of these definitions seem to indicate that all of God's revelations to us haven't yet been made. Some *mystery* may yet be revealed to us, even though *mystery* is cited many times in the New Testament.

Some of these citations are:

> *Now to him who is able to establish you by my gospel and the proclamation of Jesus Christ, according to the revelation of the mystery hidden for long ages past, but now revealed and made known through the prophetic writings by the command of the eternal God, so that all nations might believe and obey him—to the only wise God be glory forever through Jesus Christ! Amen. (Rom 16:25-27 NIV)*

> *Praise be to the God and Father of our Lord Jesus Christ, who has blessed us in the heavenly realms with every spiritual blessing in Christ.4 For he chose us in him before the creation of the world to be holy*

*and blameless in his sight. In love he predestined us to be adopted as his sons through Jesus Christ, in accordance with his pleasure and will— to the praise of his glorious grace, which he has freely given us in the One he loves. In him we have redemption through his blood, the forgiveness of sins, in accordance with the riches of God's grace that he lavished on us with all wisdom and understanding. And he made known to us the **mystery** of his will according to his good pleasure, which he purposed in Christ, to be put into effect when the times will have reached their fulfillment — to bring all things in heaven and on earth together under one head, even Christ. In him we were also chosen, having been predestined according to the plan of him who works out everything in conformity with the purpose of his will, in order that we, who were the first to hope in Christ, might be for the praise of his glory. And you also were included in Christ when you heard the word of truth, the gospel of your salvation. Having believed, you were marked in him with a seal, the promised Holy Spirit, who is a deposit guaranteeing our inheritance until the redemption of those who are God's possession — to the praise of his glory. (Eph 1:3-14 NIV)*

*Surely you have heard about the administration of God's grace that was given to me for you, that is, the **mystery** made known to me by revelation, as I have already written briefly. In reading this, then, you will be able to understand my insight into the **mystery** of Christ, which was not made known to men in other generations as it has now been revealed by the Spirit to God's holy apostles and prophets. This **mystery** is that through the gospel the Gentiles are heirs together with Israel, members together of one body, and sharers together in the promise in Christ Jesus. I became a servant of this gospel by the gift of God's grace given me through the working of his power. Although I am less*

53

*than the least of all God's people, this grace was given me: to preach to the Gentiles the unsearchable riches of Christ, and to make plain to everyone the administration of this **mystery**, which for ages past was kept hidden in God, who created all things. His intent was that now, through the church, the manifold wisdom of God should be made known to the rulers and authorities in the heavenly realms, according to his eternal purpose which he accomplished in Christ Jesus our Lord. In him and through faith in him we may approach God with freedom and confidence. I ask you, therefore, not to be discouraged because of my sufferings for you, which are your glory. (Eph 3:2-13 NIV)*

*Pray also for me, that whenever I open my mouth, words may be given me so that I will fearlessly make known the **mystery** of the gospel, 20 for which I am an ambassador in chains. Pray that I may declare it fearlessly, as I should. (Eph 6:19-20 NIV)*

*Now I rejoice in what was suffered for you, and I fill up in my flesh what is still lacking in regard to Christ's afflictions, for the sake of his body, which is the church. I have become its servant by the commission God gave me to present to you the word of God in its fullness— the **mystery** that has been kept hidden for ages and generations, but is now disclosed to the saints. To them God has chosen to make known among the Gentiles the glorious riches of this **mystery**, which is Christ in you, the hope of glory. (Col 1:24-27 NIV)*

*My purpose is that they may be encouraged in heart and united in love, so that they may have the full riches of complete understanding, in order that they may know the **mystery** of God, namely, Christ, in whom are hidden all the treasures of wisdom and knowledge. (Col 2:2-3 NIV)*

*But in the days when the seventh angel is about to sound his trumpet, the **mystery** of God will be accomplished, just as he announced to his servants the prophets. (Rev 10:7 NIV)*

Is it probable that this **mystery** is very important to God, since He inspired many of the New Testament authors to include it in their writings? Thus, shouldn't it be important to us as well?

As stated previously, in the past God has revealed Himself and His plan for us in His own way and in His own time.

Is it possible also that He is *continuing* to reveal Himself and His creation of the universe to us today and into the future? Could this be a continuing **mystery** that He will reveal to us when He is ready and when He perceives that we're ready?

Perhaps to further explain His **mystery** of creation, God tells us:

In the beginning God created the heavens and the earth. (Gen 1:1 KJV)

...the Spirit of God was hovering over the waters. (Gen 1:2 KJV)

Then God said, "Let us make man in our image, in our likeness, and let them rule over the fish of the sea and the birds of the air, over the livestock, over all the earth, and over all the creatures that move along the ground." (Gen 1:26 NIV)

In the beginning was the Word, and the Word was with God, and the Word was God. He was with God in the beginning. Through him all things were made; without him nothing was made that has been made. 4 In him was life, and that life was the light of men. The light shines in the darkness, but the darkness has not understood it. (John 1:1-5 NIV)

Where were you when I laid the earth's foundation?
Tell me, if you understand.
Who marked off its dimensions? Surely you know!
Who stretched a measuring line across it?
On what were its footings set,
or who laid its cornerstone—
while the morning stars sang together
and <u>all the angels shouted for joy</u>? (Job 38:4-7 NIV)

Praise him, all his angels,
praise him, all his heavenly hosts.
Praise him, sun and moon,
praise him, all you shining stars.
Praise him, you highest heavens
and you waters above the skies.
Let them praise the name of the Lord,
<u>for he commanded and they were created</u>.
He set them in place for ever and ever;
he gave a decree that will never pass away. (Ps 148:2-6
NIV)

Praise the Lord, <u>you his angels,</u>
<u>you mighty ones who do his bidding,</u>
<u>who obey his word.</u>
Praise the Lord<u>, all his heavenly hosts</u>,
you his servants <u>who do his will</u>. (Ps 103:20-21 NIV)

Matt 26:50-54 *Then the men stepped forward, seized Jesus and arrested him. With that, one of Jesus' companions reached for his sword, drew it out and struck the servant of the high priest, cutting off his ear.*

"Put your sword back in its place," Jesus said to him, "for all who draw the sword will die by the sword. Do you think I cannot call on my Father, and <u>he will at once put at my disposal more than twelve legions of angels</u>?

But how then would the Scriptures be fulfilled that say it must happen in this way?" (Matt 26:50-54 NIV)

(Note: Twelve *legions of angels would be between 36,000 and 72,000 angels.)*

These Scriptures, as well as the remainder of Genesis chapters 1 and 2, tell us that God the Father and Jesus the Son created the universe. The Spirit of God was there (The Holy Spirit?), as well as all the innumerable angels and heavenly hosts.

Some of the biblical accounts of the creation state that God *spoke* everything into existence. As the almighty Jehovah God, could he not have ordered or commanded (spoken) and everyone under his command then followed his orders and created the universe as he directed and gave them power? Perhaps God, as CEO of everything, simply ordered the creation and because of His majesty, power, and authority, it was done as He directed.

Were we capable in the early history of our development (like Johnny) to understand what God possibly could have revealed to us? Is God is now revealing to us more details about His creation through the study of science—chemistry, geology, paleontology, genetics, biochemistry, embryology, and on and on?

Since He created science and its many branches, is now possible to use the study of His science to begin to read, understand, and begin to solve this **mystery**? As we continue to study and better understand more of science, we find that these findings increasingly agree with each other and help to interpret, understand, and support the truths found in the Bible concerning creation.

Science can't, and never will, take the place of God! Science is just something God created when He created the universe. It shows us His power, might, and wisdom, and it helps us better understand His revelations to us, both as written in the Bible and as obtained through a study of His science. By using the discoveries of science, we can greatly improve our lives by using these wonderful revelations from a loving God who cares for each of us.

The **mystery** *of salvation* has been revealed to us through the study of the Bible. More specifically, it is explained in Christ's teachings in the New Testament. The explanation of the **mystery** *of creation* was started in the Bible, but it's *still being revealed and discovered* through the study of His creation.

CHAPTER 4

What a Study of God's Creation Reveals to Us

Don't cast a blind eye, see the *deeds* of God as well as His *words*.

Continued scientific research yields discoveries in God's creation that will clarify, explain, and advance our knowledge and understanding of God and His importance to humankind just as continued research of the Scriptures and other written words (history, Dead Sea Scrolls, ancient writings, etc.) will help clarify and interpret the Bible's teachings, support its accuracy, and further explain God's will for us.

We must constantly update ourselves in *all* of God's continuing revelations to us, whether through the study of His creation or through the study of His written Word

Some *Bible Only Believers* seem almost terrified of science and its new revelations to us. They seem to feel that the study of science will somehow diminish their concept of God, His majesty and power, and that it might even cause them to question or lose their faith in Him. *The opposite is really the truth.* New discoveries, properly done and correctly interpreted, will always show increasing evidence of the existence of God, at least to the extent He will allow them at a given time. If humankind can ever prove the existence of God, then where do Faith and Hope fit into our belief system? *Faith in God* is required for our proper relationship with Him, not *proof of God!*

As Paul said in the book of Hebrews:

> *Now <u>faith</u> is being sure of what we <u>hope</u> for and certain
> of what we do not see. This is what the ancients were
> commended for. By faith we understand that the
> universe was formed <u>at God's command, so that what
> is seen was not made out of what was visible</u>. (Heb
> 11:1-3 NIV)*

So much is said with so few words. God ordered or commanded that the universe be formed. Who and/or what did He command? Is it reasonable that the Supreme Being would command the angels and all the other heavenly hosts to *build* it? But, just what would they build it from? Where did all the matter of the entire universe come from? Most believers hold that the universe was created (made from nothing) by the Creator as stated above, "*so that what is seen was not made out of what was visible.*"

Can science ever even attempt to explain creating the universe that is seen from what was not visible? Perhaps it *can* be explained, and in so doing, it may blow one's mind.

Einstein's theory of relativity indicates that matter and energy can be inter-converted. That is, energy can become matter, and matter can become energy through the formula:

$$e = mc^2$$

Or, in words, the formula states:

energy = mass x the speed of light x the speed of light

Using this formula, if God created all the mass of the universe by this means, then He had the *invisible* power or energy to form all that inconceivably immense *visible* mass. This power or energy can be calculated by multiplying the mass of the *entire* universe by the speed of light (186,000 miles per second), and this number multiplied again by the speed of light (186,000 miles per second).

It's seemingly impossible for anyone except a trained physicist to even begin to comprehend the immense values involved in applying Einstein's equation to the creative process.

We might begin our attempt to understand this difficult concept by considering for a moment that the energy released when a bullet, weighing less than an ounce and traveling a few thousand feet per second, can literally explode a watermelon when it hits it.

Going one step further, let's consider the energy released when an automobile weighing a few thousand pounds and moving sixty miles per hour (eighty-eight feet per second) hits a solid concrete barrier so that it comes to a complete and immediate stop and all the energy of that momentum is instantaneously released. No doubt the car would be *totaled* through the release of that energy.

Going some steps further, what if that car were moving at 1,000 miles per hour? Or, 1,000 miles per second? Or 186,000 miles per second and *multiplied again* by 186,000? How much energy would that involve if it were instantaneously released? Can you see a mushroom cloud forming as a result of that impact?

Now consider that the object traveling at that immense speed had the mass of our moon, or had the mass of our sun, or the mass of our galaxy, or the mass of *all* the matter in the universe? Is it possible to even begin to comprehend that amount of energy?

If God created the universe from nothing by this process, then according to Einstein's formula He had the power, force, and energy of all the mass of the universe times the speed of light times the speed of light again.

Are you beginning to see the power or energy involved? That's the power required to form the mass of the universe. And, this illustration is just a *portion* of the total power of *our* God!

Wow! Talk about an *almighty* and *all-powerful* God and Creator! And, we can be sure that He probably didn't even *work up a sweat* in the whole process of creation. How much more power and might did He have *beyond* that involved in the creative process? And, just how much power and energy does He still have? Does science and scripture work hand in hand to help us understand God? Does it give an indication of Gods limitless power and knowledge to be able to create all the matter in the entire universe? *You bet it does!*

But, just creating all that matter does not even begin to explain *how* it was all *put together*, that is, how everything in the entire universe was assembled in an orderly, functioning manner, from the largest and most distant galaxies, down to the smallest subatomic particles present in every bit of that material. Who, except God, could possibly have had the wisdom and ability to create all that matter from nothing and organize it into such an incredibly complex creation? Yet, He did it, *and* He has kept it functioning properly from the beginning, up to the present, and on into the indefinite future.

If there's a creation, there must've been a Creator! Or, in a more modern vernacular, if there was a *big bang*, then there must have been a *Big Banger!* Things as massive and intricate as the universe just can't appear spontaneously.

One can't observe all the created things in the universe and not believe that *someone* was responsible for their creation and existence. Houses don't appear unless someone builds them. Jet liners don't appear unless they're manufactured. The myriad of life forms didn't originate unless they were made. The same is true for the universe. We can't *prove* the existence of God short of meeting Him face-to-face in the next life, but we can *increasingly strengthen our faith* in Him by studying and learning about His creation.

Accurate discoveries and advancements in science will always serve to glorify God and illustrate to us His power and majesty. Because He is always truthful in all His revelations to us, we can be assured that new discoveries, properly obtained, interpreted, and understood, will be in accordance with His divine will and plan. *We shouldn't fear new discoveries, but embrace them as new revelations from God to us.* We should, however, be concerned and alert, making sure that these findings are obtained, interpreted, and used properly according to His will and for His glorification. We should observe God's principles and teachings in His Bible and make sure that we're using these things correctly, so that these new discoveries can, and will be, used for the benefit of humankind and to the glory of God.

When they're used improperly, God is not glorified and humankind is not helped, but often harmed.

God does not lie to us or mislead us. It's our responsibility to study and *properly* interpret everything He makes available to us as a continuing revelation of His Mystery according to His timetable. We won't receive all of it today or tomorrow, nor will we properly interpret it today or tomorrow. It's an *ongoing* process that we can only hope to begin to achieve through much work, study, meditation, and prayer. After all, "Who can know the mind of God?"

Remember that when God sent his Son to earth as a savior for humankind, He was not accepted by or believed in by His own. They were expecting someone else—a mighty king, not an infant born in an animal stable in a small village. Are we keeping an open mind to receive God's continuing revelations to us, or are we (like those in Jesus' day) taking the easier and more comfortable position of retaining our current concepts of Him and ignoring new revelations because they're difficult to understand or are contrary to our beliefs?

Are we "studying" and "rightly dividing the word of truth" as the Bible directs in *2 Tim 2:15*? Are we studying and analyzing correctly *everything* God has given us through His written Word *as well as* the physical evidence He left during His process of creation?

The continuing study and research of all of God's revelations to us, whether through His written Word or through the scientific observation of His creation, will always increase our understanding of Him and His plan for humankind. We need to use *all* of His revelations in order to get a better knowledge of Him and His plan for us. These studies will never diminish our need for Him, but they'll enhance and strengthen our faith in Him, our reverence for Him, and the recognition of our dependence on Him.

He made us, gave us life, and gave us a plan to use so that we could be able to live for eternity in heaven with Him. He did all of that for us. But *why* would He do that for us? Could it be that He loves us? **God is love!** How much do we love God? Do we love Him enough to study and to try to understand *everything* we can about Him and His plan for our lives? Do we *do* everything He commands?

The more we learn and understand about how God made the universe the stronger our faith should become - - *not* the reverse.

To a student of biology, there's nothing more miraculous and astonishing than following the wonderfully beautiful transition of a fertilized egg (whether of a lower vertebrate animal or a human being) through the many stages of progressive growth and development. It's an amazing sight to witness, let alone to try to understand. Just *how* does the genetic material contained in the fertilized egg direct the whole orderly process to form the wonderfully developed embryo and eventually the mature adult being. It compares extremely well with the process described in the evolutionary process observed in the development of lower forms of life into higher forms. There is *no way* these parallel developments could occur unless someone (God) used very careful planning and supreme knowledge of science to accomplish these feats. The author is at a loss to *understand why we do not use more science in our churches and Sunday school classes to show the overwhelming evidence of God's existence.* This application is true, not only in biology, but in the other fields of science as well.

We must remember that the younger people of today are much better educated in science and technology than the older adults. Just look around at how many of these young people have the latest in electronic gadgets and know very well how to use them. They're so dependent on these gadgets, they simply wouldn't leave home without them. Compare this phenomenon with the number of young people who carry a Bible with them on a daily basis or even read and study the Bible regularly. Sadly, most of them know more about these gadgets, that will be outdated and obsolete in a few months or years, than they know about the Bible, which will *never* become outdated. ***How sad!***

I'm afraid that if we fail to teach that the God of the Bible is also the God of all scientific knowledge, it may lead to their loss of faith in the God of the Bible. But, ***He is one and the same!*** As previously stated, some recent studies show that about 70 per cent of the young people in our churches today will leave the church sometime in their later lives. Could this be the reason for their leaving? How many older people leave for the same or similar reason? ***What a tragedy!***

What can/should we do to reverse this process? Shouldn't we use *everything* we have available to us to try to teach our young (and older) people about God?

Perhaps the more important question is, "Will we?"

<u>**Where are we now in today's world?**</u>

In the recent past, humankind has gained a tremendous amount of knowledge by pursuing investigations into God's scientific world. We've split the atom, traveled to the moon and back, explored the solar system and beyond using spacecraft, cracked the DNA code, mapped the genetics of humans, produced test tube babies, corrected birth defects in infants, developed many life-saving medicines, eradicated small pox, greatly reduced the incidences of polio, traveled faster than the speed of sound, and developed electronic knowledge be able to make and use computers, cell phones, GPS navigation. The list is seemingly endless. It's very important to remember that all of this has been revealed to us as a result of our investigation into God's creation, and what He has allowed us to discover.

Is He finished revealing His ***mystery*** to us? What will we discover tomorrow? Next year? In ten years? In this century? As has been said many times by many individuals, "Only God knows!" Whatever it is, I'm sure it's going to be according to His will and beyond our wildest imaginations.

Shouldn't we be prepared to be surprised? What if He allows us to find life in other parts of the universe? Or, what if He allows us to place DNA molecules from an extinct dinosaur into an appropriate egg cytoplasm and hatch a real live dinosaur? Or what if He allows us to assemble the necessary chemical components to make a primitive life form?

I remember Buck Rogers from my youth and the "impossible" things he could do in the many fictitious stories written about him. Now, just a few decades later, humans have been able to do most, if not all, of the things he did.

Is it possible that today we are in a Buck Rogers world imagining doing similar, relatively impossible feats in our future? If we do achieve some of these seemingly impossible feats, and many people believe that it will happen, *how will it affect our belief in God?*

For some, it may simply be a further discovery of God's wonderful power, wisdom, and love for us and His creation. It will further reinforce their faith and allow a better understanding of Him and His plan for all of us. Others may accept these discoveries as some did when the moon landing occurred. They refused to believe it, just as some today still believe the earth is flat. They claimed that the moon landing was all done by a bunch of actors in a sound stage in Hollywood, and that some high government officials took the money budgeted for the project and put it in their own bank accounts. In spite of all the evidence to the contrary, in their minds they believed it never really happened.

Still others may take the example of the ostrich that buries its head in the sand and ignores the whole thing, thus feeling safe in spite of the events actually taking place. These individuals may bury their heads in *their interpretation* of the Bible (their sand) and ignore what is actually happening because it makes them feel uncomfortable or challenges what they believe. They may also be afraid that it will weaken *their* faith. Some are doing this today with a number of our scientific findings.

CHAPTER 5

What Paul Teaches Us in Romans

> *For what can be known about God is plain to them, because God has shown it to them.* Ever since the creation of the world his eternal power and divine nature, invisible though they are, have been understood and seen through the things he has made. So they are without excuse; for though they knew God, they did not honor him as God or give thanks to him, but they became futile in their thinking, and their senseless minds were darkened. (Rom 1:19-22 RSV)

We believe that the Bible relates to us today just as it did when it was written. Since we do believe this, then might we say that verse 19 *could* read as follows?

> *For what can be known about God is plain to them* **and to us***, because God has shown it to them,* **and is showing it to us day by day in ever increasing detail***.*

Just consider for a moment how much more we know and understand God's creation *today* than when Paul wrote his letter to the Romans. How much more is this knowledge revealing to us the *eternal power and divine nature* of God? And, we continue to study God's marvelous creation and learn more about it every day.

If we fail to use this tremendous treasure God has given us, we're losing a very convincing teaching/learning principle, especially with the scientifically literate and tech-savvy young people of today. Unfortunately, much of what they've been taught is done by increasing numbers of agnostic and atheistically-leaning teachers. Indeed, most public school systems forbid or suppress teaching of the Bible and any correlation between science and the Bible.

It's also unfortunate that most of the teachers in churches today aren't educated enough in science to be able to properly teach and emphasize the wonderful correlations between the God of the Bible and the *same* God of science. What a loss of opportunity! A loss that may never be available again in the lifetimes of the students in these classes.

I've observed so many times that the failure to educate the young properly in the wonderful *relationships between* the Bible and science results in the put down of scientific and technological learning. This is evident to the extent that the young will begin to question which is true--the interpretations of the Bible as presented by some of their Bible school teachers or their increasingly greater knowledge of science and its provability.

Thus, these very confused young people grow to adulthood and fail to see or understand all of the eternal power and divine nature of God. Unfortunately, they and their teachers have not

> *understood and seen through the things he has made.*
> *So they are without excuse; for though they knew God,*
> *they did not honor him as God or give thanks to him, but*
> *they became futile in their thinking, and their senseless*
> *minds were darkened. (Romans 1:20-21 NRSV)*

To me, one of the saddest things happening in today's churches and other places of learning, is that the teachers and preachers aren't willing to study and learn what God's creation *can* teach us. They just want to hold tightly to their anti-science, Bible-only beliefs they've grown so comfortable with for most of their lives. They seem to be afraid that, by knowing more of science, it will somehow weaken or destroy their faith *in their interpretation* of the Bible, when just the opposite should be the case. Thus, they shun any exposure to this knowledge and anyone and everyone who possess any understanding and belief in scientific knowledge. They openly admit that they don't know very much about science, saying, "I'll just stay with the Bible." Perhaps another way of stating heir position is, "I'll stay with *my interpretation* of the Bible." They're missing completely the very wonderful insight into the power, majesty, and wisdom of God that He makes available through the study of His science, what it can teach us, and how it can help in our understanding of the Bible and of God.

Is this is what God wants? Isn't this *exactly* the same opposition Jesus, John the Baptist, the Apostles, and disciples faced in the first century when the religious leaders of that time held so firmly to *their interpretation* of Scripture and refused to believe the new teachings of Jesus? Then, what about the God's new teachings He gives us through the study of His creation?

These concepts cast enormous stumbling blocks to today's youth (and many adults as well). Learning about God through Bible study alone, and avoiding what God is telling us through the study of his creation, would be like teaching the Bible but omitting the book of Acts, or the gospels, or the letters, or Revelation, or the Old Testament. We shouldn't teach just *part* of what God has revealed to us, yet this is happening every day in almost every church and church classroom.

Another very serious outcome of Bible-only teaching (avoiding or omitting God's scientific revelations to us) is its effect on the scientifically literate individuals who may be deficient in Bible knowledge. They desperately *need* God's influence as taught in biblical Scripture. Imagine the effect on these individuals when they attend a church that preaches and teaches that science (and God's science at that) is not proven and may even be a work of the Devil and thus has no place in today's Christian beliefs.

Some anti-science leaders use various erroneous illustrations of science in a very mocking manner, thereby intending to prove their beliefs and viewpoints and belittle those beliefs held by the scientifically literate. Their plan is to give a comedic type of entertainment, resulting in laughter and ready acceptance of their views by their audiences. Actually, they're really just exposing their lack of scientific knowledge and probably are discouraging the science-oriented individuals in their audience from wanting to hear more of their teaching and preaching about Christ and His plan for their salvation. Is this really the result they should be seeking?

Some people today doubt the accuracy of Carbon-14 dating but gladly use radiation from Cobalt 60 when they have cancer and are desperately seeking a cure. They fail to acknowledge the millions of lives saved through the scientific development of polio vaccine, small pox vaccine, and the myriad of antibiotics. Millions have been saved from starvation by increased food production through the hybridization of crops, the advances in the use of fertilizers and soil science, the use of insecticides to save crops from destruction, the use of preservatives and better methods of food storage to prevent spoilage. They don't always realize that knowledge about water pollution and the sanitary disposal of waste water can prevent *E. coli*, typhoid, and many other deadly infections. They ignore the use of the science of chemistry to make synthetic fibers to form clothing, the use of petroleum to make transportation possible, and the use of DNA testing to prove the guilt or innocence of imprisoned individuals. The list is endless. But, could these and the many, many other things we've learned from the study of God's science have anything at all to do with what Jesus spoke about in this Scripture?

> *For I was <u>hungry</u> and you gave me something to eat, I was <u>thirsty</u> and you gave me something to drink, I was a stranger and you invited me in, I needed clothes and you <u>clothed</u> me, I was <u>sick</u> and you <u>looked after</u> me, I was in prison and you <u>came to visit</u> me.' (Matt 25:35-36 NIV)*

These non-science individuals use all of the modern advances God's science has given us, yet, they seemingly can't or won't accept the fact that the same science tells us volumes about God's creative process. The scientifically inclined are probably wondering, *"Just how hypocritical can you get? Picking and choosing what you **want** to believe rather than trying to study and understand **all** of God's knowledge He is revealing to us."*

Is it any wonder that many scientifically-inclined individuals are turned off by this and lose interest in churches that have and teach this mind-set? Most tragic of all is the previously mentioned fact that 70 per cent or more of the young people brought up in today's churches will leave the church sometime in their later lives. Why? Today's youth are not dummies, they realize that instead of using *all* of God's revelations to us, some individuals seem to be using *only part* of God's revelations to us, and they're *using only their interpretations* of that revelation. This perception leaves the impression that if you don't agree with us, then perhaps you would be better off going elsewhere, or maybe even not going to any church because you'll probably only cause discord wherever you go. It throws up an impenetrable wall around *our well-studied, established, and consequently infallible* interpretation of the Bible and our lack of concern for or knowledge about the *rest* of God's revelations to us.

One of the biggest problems with avoiding science is the impression such ignorance gives to the more scientifically literate individuals in the churches. How they may see those Bible only individuals, who chose to ignore science and the revelations God is giving us, might be illustrated by the following comparison:

> The scientifically illiterate individuals who ignore science could be compared to a person who has studied neither Greek or Hebrew and who only has access to a Hebrew Old Testament and a Greek New Testament. Just how much of the information in either testament could this individual read, understand, teach, and explain if all they knew of the two languages were their alphabets and perhaps the meaning of a few words of each language?

The same is true with science. If one hasn't studied science and doesn't understand the terminology and language, then how can he/she possibly understand the principles involved? Believe me, it's impossible even to *begin* to understand some of the complexities God has revealed to us through our study of his marvelous creation if one knows only the "alphabet" and the meaning of a few words of science.

Many scientifically oriented individuals who visit churches with the Bible only mind-set won't be impressed. Indeed, they're probably turned off by what they may hear, because they see a great problem with that viewpoint. At best, they'll still keep their faith in the Creator, but won't be much more than lukewarm in their church activities. At worst, they'll move completely away from the church, their belief in God, become either agnostic or completely atheistic, and *reap the consequences of this action.*

It's extremely unfortunate when many of these individuals become teachers and professors and gain great influence over others, especially our young people. With the degree of academic freedom present in today's schools, colleges, and universities they can, and many times will, take great delight in ridiculing and shooting down any young person's religious beliefs whenever the opportunity arises. And, since they're in control of the topics of discussion, they *can and will* create many opportunities to do so.

In the college or university setting, this critical event occurs at a particularly vulnerable point in the young person's life. The students probably have just left the controlled oversight and discipline of their parents and are experiencing peer pressure greater than any other time in their lives. Their college professors probably have been teaching the same material for many years and know almost everything about the subjects they teach. This highly educated appearance is very impressive, even godlike, to the young students who regard their teachers as *knowing everything.* This impression on their students can even hide the professor's lack of biblical knowledge and deficiency of his/her religious beliefs. Regrettably the students' upbringing, parental teachings, and religious influences are often reduced or even destroyed as a result.

If only *these* teachers had been reached earlier and had their spiritual lives set on a God-oriented course. What a difference that might have made! But, how could this have been done?

Do any ideas come to mind?

Did *they* fail God, or did *we* fail them? What should *we* have done differently that might have prevented this extremely unfortunate mindset? And what about the students who're led to believe the same as their professors and teachers? How will they influence their friends and what will they teach *their* children? These problems can go on and on into a vicious cycle. It's been said that the good or bad influences of the parents and teachers can affect many future generations.

For someone to say that he/she spent an afternoon in a Natural History Museum observing the displays on evolution is grossly short of learning enough about *some* of the principles of evolution to even *begin* to form an opinion about the *whole concept*. This is even more clearly illustrated when those individuals come away believing that the display teaches that man came from monkey--a completely erroneous conclusion. That's not at all what evolution is about. By comparison, if you were to ask those persons how long it took them to learn a foreign language, algebra, calculus, accounting, the tax code, the Bible, music theory, dentistry, medicine, nursing, engineering or any of a myriad of other topics, they certainly couldn't say they could obtain a good grasp of knowledge of the subject in an afternoon visit to a museum.

I've studied science and evolution and the Bible for over sixty years and have found wonderful revelations of the brilliance, power, majesty, and wisdom of God. During my twenty-plus years of college and university teaching experience, I've learned that it takes at least three middle- to upper-level college science courses and their pre-requisites even to *begin* to expose enough material to my students for them to visualize and understand a small part of the beautiful mosaic of God's creation that extends from one end of space to the other. It's impossible for any human to comprehend all of just one small part (biology, chemistry, astronomy, etc.) let alone all of each of these areas of study.

Only God has done that!

Just imagine how marvelous God is. *He knows it all*, and what's even more marvelous, *He made it all*. If we ignore the marvels God is revealing to us daily, we're missing a wonderfully powerful tool for teaching about God and His plan for each of us.

God has continuously revealed Himself and His desires for us since the creation. Is He finished with his revelations to us, or is He continuing to reveal Himself in an unexpected manner as we study His creation in increasingly greater detail? Shouldn't we use these discoveries to more fully understand and realize that we <u>must</u>:

> *Love and honor him as God and give thanks to him".*
> *(Romans 1:21 NRSV)*

Loving and honoring God and giving thanks to Him is God's greatest commandment to us. Yet, we are missing what could be one of the strongest evidences of the existence and purpose of God if we ignore what He is revealing to through the study of His creation. Why don't we use this evidence, not only to strengthen our faith in God, but to help others *build their faith* in God? This would give us the wonderful opportunity help us and others to accomplish this most important goal.

Please, let's don't be without excuse as it says in Romans 1:19 - 22.

CHAPTER 6

Where Should We Go From Here?

Hopefully, the reader can now begin to realize that the study of the written Word and the study of the universe are true revelations from God to humankind. *How could they not be messages from God?* He gave them to us for our use, and although our knowledge of them is ever-increasing, we can never completely know or understand all of God's knowledge or wisdom. *Our knowledge of His creation will never replace our need for Him, nor will it ever reduce His majesty and power. It can only increase the awareness of our dependence on Him!*

I was raised in a very conservative Restoration Movement church. The Bible lessons I learned during my youth have stayed with me throughout my adult life. However, being keenly interested in science, I soon became aware of the "conflicts" between science and religion. I read many articles basically entitled The Bible vs. Evolution, The Bible vs. Science, or similar wording. Many of these forced the concept that one must choose either the Bible or science. *There was no middle ground.* You couldn't live with one hand in the Bible and the other hand in a science book. Some even seemed to expound that all scientific knowledge is the work of the Devil and should be shunned completely. It's interesting to note that these individuals use the discoveries of science to enhance their lifestyles: electronic technology (computers, tv, cell phones, GPS navigation, etc.); transportation (automobiles, airplanes, space travel); creature-comfort items (air conditioning, washing machines, dishwashers, microwave ovens, etc.); and labor-saving devices (tractors, trucks, power mowers, power tools, and on and on).

If it had not been for the use of science and the many wonderful things it has given us to use, I wonder *how many of us would be alive today*?

Many don't seem to understand that all of these revelations from God were made possible through the study of His creation and through the proper understanding and application of these findings. The principles are made possible through the use of the scientific method,--the *same principle* that's led to the many conclusions and theories some judge to be against their interpretations of the Bible.

Some say, "After all, a lot of science is just theory, and it hasn't been and can't be proven." However, they must be convinced of the accuracy of the theories of avionics since they repeatedly fly from one city to another. They welcome the use of antibiotics and other medications to treat infections and diseases such as diabetes, high blood pressure, low basal metabolic rate, thyroid disorders, cancer and its treatment; corrective surgeries, anemia, and immunizations. The list is endless.

Some continue by saying, "Since the age of the universe can't be proven to *our* satisfaction to be more than a few thousand years old, and since the theory of evolution can't be proven, we'll stick with the Bible." What they don't realize is they are sticking with *their interpretation* of it, which may not be completely accurate in how God intended for us to interpret it today. They then smile with satisfaction, assuming that their knowledge and understanding is essentially complete and accurate, and that they are correct in their conclusions. They seemingly pat themselves on their backs for having a very strong faith that can withstand attacks from the evil one(s) who are attempting to weaken or destroy their faith, but who, in fact, may be trying to educate them about *all* of God's revelations to humankind.

If they're queried further about the age of the universe as revealed using the scientific method, it's demonstrated that their knowledge is biased, incomplete, and many times inaccurate. Their concept of the theory of evolution is that it teaches that man descended from monkeys, which is completely inaccurate. Yet, for the most part, they're *not aware* of their lack of the knowledge revealed by the study of God's creation and are seemingly uninterested in pursuing their education of it. They feel that the Bible, as they interpret it, will tell them everything they need to know, regardless of what a study of God's creation tells us.

Some individuals even contend that evolution cannot be proven because it can't be repeated like a lab experiment. This idea appears to be something they feel is extremely necessary for absolute proof of a theory. Can these individuals prove they were born by being born again? Can they prove that last year happened by repeating it?

As presented earlier, one might compare their knowledge of science with a person speaking only English trying to explain his/ her beliefs using just the Hebrew Old Testament and the Greek New Testament and knowing only the alphabets and a few words of each language. They simply aren't qualified or knowledgeable enough to do the job. Even if they do try to understand and explain their concept of science and what it teaches, consider how many science courses *they* may have taken: Geology? Chemistry? Astronomy? Genetics? Anatomy? Paleontology? Embryology? Comparative Anatomy? Biochemistry? Immunology? Zoology? Archeology? Metabolism? Protein Synthesis? Enzymology? Botany? Physiology? Endocrinology? Physics? Archaeology? Just how qualified are they?

We must remember that there are great differences among scientists because of the vastly different fields of science each has studied. Some of them are quite knowledgeable about *their* specific area of science, but have no education or study in a completely different discipline. For example, astrophysicists may be experts in their field, but may have no insight into paleontology or molecular biology. As a result, they may make erroneous conclusions in areas *outside their area of expertise.* We must carefully examine what different people say about a topic as well as how much they *know* about it and *how qualified* they are to offer an opinion.

The point I'm trying to make here is that if you ask anyone what they *think* about a certain scientific topic, they may speak volumes. However, if you ask them what they actually *know* about that same topic, you may not get much of a response at all.

As I've written previously, many science-deficient individuals say that they will stick with their Bible. What they're actually saying is that they will stick with *their interpretation* of the Bible and, unfortunately, ignore everything else they don't know or understand. Is everyone's interpretation of the Bible the same? Which interpretation is the correct one? Isn't this the main reason why there are so many different beliefs, denominations, and churches? Does each one's interpretation remain the same throughout one's lifetime, or do changes occur? Do you believe the same now as when you first began studying the Bible? Which of your beliefs were correct?

Should we be most concerned with our *current interpretation* of Scripture, or should we seek what God *meant* in the Scriptures He has given us? Shouldn't we utilize *all* of God's revelations to us, biblical as well as scientific, in seeking Him and discovering and knowing His will for our lives and what we should teach others about Him?

It's only fair to mention here that not all scientists agree on everything, just as all preachers, teachers, and church leaders don't agree on everything. There are good and bad scientists just as there are good and bad religious leaders. Just because there is a bad one in a group doesn't mean we should condemn the whole group.

It has been said that "History repeats itself". If we look back at the life of Christ, we find that His birth, life, death, and resurrection were predicted many times in the Old Testament. Yet, when God chose to reveal *His Mystery* and send his Son as our Savior, the Jews weren't ready for Him and refused to accept it. John's Gospel describes it so well.

> *In the beginning was the Word, and the Word was with God, and the Word was God. He was with God in the beginning. Through him all things were made; without*

*him nothing was made that has been made. In him was life, and that life was the light of men. The light shines in the darkness, **but the darkness has not understood it**.*

There came a man who was sent from God; his name was John. He came as a witness to testify concerning that light, so that through him all men might believe. He himself was not the light; he came only as a witness to the light. The true light that gives light to every man was coming into the world.

*He was in the world, and though the world was made through him, **the world did not recognize him**. He came to that which was his own, **but his own did not receive him**. Yet to all who received him, to those who believed in his name, he gave the right to become children of God— children born not of natural descent, nor of human decision or a husband's will, but born of God.*

The Word became flesh and made his dwelling among us. We have seen his glory, the glory of the One and Only, who came from the Father, full of grace and truth. (John 1 1-14 NIV)

If the findings in our study of the universe are revelations from God to us today, is it also possible that there are some now that won't *understand* or *recognize* them as revelations from God to us? *Is this history repeating itself?* If we study the New Testament, we find that most of Jesus' and the apostles' time was spent trying to convince the religious leaders of that day to understand, accept, believe, and teach that Jesus was the prophesied Savior of humankind, a very new and different concept than what they'd believed for so long.

The concepts presented in this book have been excruciatingly formulated over many decades of careful thought and study. I vividly remember my past struggles of being encouraged, and, sometimes even forced, to choose between my love of the study of science and my love of the study of the Bible. I was assured that there was no acceptable middle ground and that if that middle point of view were chosen, I would be lukewarm in my belief and The Book of Revelation tells us what God does with "lukewarm" believers (Rev. 3:16). Over the years, My family and I have been "spewed out of the mouth" of several churches for my views. Although it hurt deeply at the time, the lingering pain came from *my inability* to properly explain, teach, and convince those churches and their leaders about the unity and support the Bible and science have with each other. This book is finally my effort to try to get most of my thoughts and beliefs in one place, hopefully to present a convincing treatise on the **unity** of the Bible and science.

In closing, let's consider again the two following Scriptures:

> *But if anyone causes one of these little ones who believe in me to sin, it would be better for him to have a large millstone hung around his neck and to be drowned in the depths of the sea. (Matt 18:6 NIV)*

> *And if anyone causes one of these little ones who believe in me to sin, it would be better for him to be thrown into the sea with a large millstone tied around his neck. (Mark 9:42 NIV)*

In light of these two Scriptures, perhaps the most challenging thing in writing this book is my concern about being inaccurate in what I've written and in doing no harm to any believer's faith. I sincerely fear and tremble at the thought of doing either or both of them.

However, I feel I must present these thoughts because I believe that, in today's world, God is recognizing our *need* for new revelations and is showing us more and more evidence of His existence, and, as a result, His loving plan for us as described in His Bible.

We need this *new approach* because the young people of today are being overwhelmed with erroneous concepts that are being taught with increasingly convincing force. Today, Bible study is being reduced to the point of complete absence in many of our homes. If the studies showing that 70 percent of the youth in today's Christian homes will leave the church at some point in their lifetime are accurate, and if this trend continues, we're approaching bankruptcy of the churches in terms of strength of faith, membership, attendance, and influence in the community. These losses are miniscule when compared to the *unmeasurable value of the souls* of those abandoning their religious faith and duty to God. We're *not* glorifying God and saving souls if *we* allow this trend to continue.

The big question is, *"**Why** are they leaving?"* I believe one of the main causes is the overwhelmingly convincing evidence and provability of scientific discoveries as compared to the decreasing emphasis on the Bible and its' study. When many of today's church leaders fail to see, understand, and teach the **unity** of the Bible and science, then what results should we expect? Then, if the youth of today are forced to choose between the two, is it any wonder they begin to question their religious teachings, lose faith, and begin leaving the church? Who can blame them? Who's at fault here? *As believers, **it's our fault**.*

What we need is **revival**. Revival in the concept that God *is* all-powerful, all-knowing, all-loving, and that He *has purpose* in and for our lives. I believe one of the better ways to accomplish this *revival* is through the proper use and teaching of ***all*** of God's revelation. If we continue doing what we're doing now, we'll continue to obtain the same results we're getting now.

I fervently hope and pray that these writings have somehow helped you in your search to more fully know God and His will and His plan for your present life and future life.

As Paul has written,

> *Therefore, my dear friends, as you have always obeyed*
> *— not only in my presence, but now much more in my*
> *absence — **continue to work out your salvation with***
> ***fear and trembling,** for it is God who works in you to*

> will and to act according to his good purpose. (Phil
> 2;12-13 NIV)

We must *continually* seek God and His will in our lives and seek to know *everything* He has revealed to us and is *still revealing* to us. In the past, many have had the attitude "The Bible is all I know and the Bible is all I need to know." This may be true as far as your own personal salvation is concerned, but will you be able to influence atheistic or agnostic individuals to a belief in God, Christ, and the Holy Spirit or will you turn them off through an attitude of indifference and ignorance of the revelations God has given us through the Bible and a study of His wonderful creation?

It's very easy and comforting to us to keep our long-held beliefs and biblical interpretations. After all, we've studied very diligently and believe that we've finally succeeded in learning everything we need to know about certain topics. However, we must remember that this is the mind-set the religious leaders had when Jesus walked the earth and brought us the completely new covenant of Christianity. Are we now being shown increasingly convincing evidence of the presence and omnipotence of God through the study of nature? Or, could it be that:

> He was in the world, and though the world was made
> through him, **the world did not recognize him.** He
> came to that which was his own, but **his own did not
> receive him.** Yet to all who received him, to those
> who believed in his name, he gave the right to become
> children of God—children born not of natural descent,
> nor of human decision or a husband's will, but born of
> God. (John 1:10-13 NIV)

Everything God reveals to us is true. Therefore:

> Finally, be strong in the Lord and in his mighty power.
> Put on the **full** armor of God so that you can take your
> stand against the devil's schemes. For our struggle

82

*is not against flesh and blood, but against the rulers, against the authorities, against the powers of this dark world and against the spiritual forces of evil in the heavenly realms. Therefore put on the full armor of God, so that when the day of evil comes, you may be able to stand your ground, and after you have done everything, to stand.4 Stand firm then, with the **belt of truth** buckled around your waist, with the breastplate of righteousness in place, and with your feet fitted with the readiness that comes from the gospel of peace. In addition to all this, take up the shield of faith, with which you can extinguish all the flaming arrows of the evil one. Take the helmet of salvation and the sword of the Spirit, which is the word of God. (Ephesians 6:10-17 NIV)*

What's included in the **belt of truth**? Is it everything God has revealed to us, or just what he has revealed to us in the Bible? Should we try to learn and understand the Bible as well as everything we can from the study of God's creation? The study of the creation doesn't teach us salvation, but it certainly does teach us that there had to be a very powerful creator. Thus, we should hear and heed what He has to say to us in His Bible. The plan for living in a good relationship to glorify God, seeking our salvation, is found only in the Bible, but we find overwhelmingly convincing evidence of His existence and power in the study of his creation.

As Paul wrote:

*Though I am free and belong to no man, **I make myself a slave to everyone**, to win as many as possible. To the Jews I became like a Jew, to win the Jews. To those under the law I became like one under the law (though I myself am not under the law), so as to win those under the law. To those not having the law I became like one not having the law (though I am not free from God's law but am under Christ's law), so as to win those not having the law. To the weak I became weak, to win the*

> weak. **I have become all things to all men so that by**
> **all possible means I might save some.** *I do all this for*
> *the sake of the gospel, that I may share in its blessings.*
> *(I Cor. 9:19-23 NIV)*

A Challenge to Christians of Today:

As Paul became all things to all people, shouldn't Christians of today *at least try* to be all things to all of today's people? Jesus could speak to all His followers, regardless of their spiritual condition or walk of life. How many of today's religious leaders (ministers, teachers, and members) can effectively speak to those who know only science and very little about the Bible? Many times, however, these science oriented persons may know much more about the Bible than the religious leaders know about science and thus the Bible teacher's job is even more difficult.

Can these leaders effectively present biblical teachings to an atheist or agnostic with any hope of bringing them to an understanding of and belief in Christ? Or, do they alienate these individuals because they don't even begin to know or understand the basic principles of God's marvelous creation? It's even sadder when some of these individuals show no interest in learning about it.

Unfortunately, many of these science only individuals, who are turned off by religious leaders deficient in the knowledge of science, become teachers in public educational institutions and can, because of academic freedom, wreak havoc with the minds of their young God-believing students. Some of these teachers and professors even seem to take delight in this process because they feel that they're somehow getting back at religious teachers who attempted to correct them and teach them things contrary to the proven principles of science about which they knew so little.

And thus the *needless* feud continues. It's a vicious circle that goes on and on. Isn't this something that needs to be overcome?

84

Is it impossible to correlate God's truth He presented in the Scriptures with the truth He presents in the study of His creation? Yes, it is because all of God's truth is absolute and infallible.

How and *by whom* will it be done? **Whose responsibility is it to correctly interpret God's word of truth?**

But, perhaps the most important question of all is...

What <u>will</u> happen if nothing is done?

The Solution

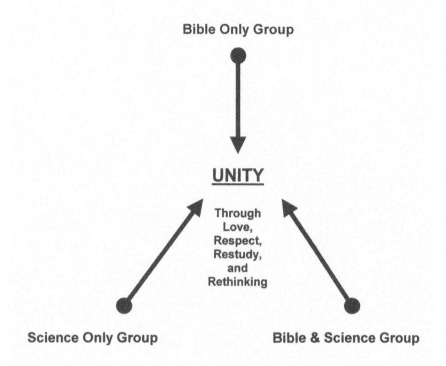

Bible Only Group

UNITY

Through
Love,
Respect,
Restudy,
and
Rethinking

Science Only Group

Bible & Science Group

What's needed is for each group to move from a confrontational mind-set to one of love, respect, restudy, and rethinking of our beliefs and knowledge so that **UNITY** can be achieved. By doing this, we can make a united attack on Satan and his efforts to place **OPPOSITION** between us that can divide us and conquer us. After all, and most importantly, isn't this what God wants from His children--for us to be united in our service and praise to Him and in our fight against Satan?